Upon realizing that my baby daughter would one day read this, I re-examined every word. To the most beautiful girl on earth – Daddy loves you.

Preface

I began having serious thoughts pertaining to the dynamics of Black romantic relationships in college upon traveling to Atlanta and conversing for hours with Spelman College's exceptional Black women. It was like the television show *A Different World.* While my reason for routinely making the two hour trip from my college was to convince a particular one of these women that she was to be my wife, it became clear that a unique dynamic was on the horizon. Many of the educated Black women I encountered had confidence in their academic and professional journey, but lacked clarity on whether enough educated Black men with at least an ounce of swagger shared their dream of creating a formidable family. It was a fair question then, and remains a growing dilemma affecting educated Black women today.

Since that time I have consistently spoken with Brothers, Sisters, family members, friends, and others about the challenges facing Black relationships. Those conversations have inspired me to share my humble thoughts for anyone willing to indulge me. As you read beyond the passion of my words, hopefully sincerity and love will be visible, along with a creative spirit that you find interesting enough to continue the exposé. Expect to see the tremendous influences of film & television, hip-hop, fiction, non-fiction, humor, politics, scholarship, and of course God as significant portions of my writings. All of these play a vital role in how Black relationships have taken shape. I will italicize significant titles within these genres at times to emphasize them as materials worthy of consideration for your repertoire. With that said, you may read a few tangents, but there is usually a method to my madness.

This book is composed of short-letters and short-stories. The format came about because I often jot down my personal reflections here and there. My thoughts were not necessarily meant for mass production, but here we are. I am an equal opportunity writer. You will find that some sections are speaking to Black men; and I do hope that you will pass these letters on to a few. Because at the end of the day it is about us, Black women and Black men, taking a deeper look at how we can do better together.

Dear Ms. Educated Black Woman is focused on a specific group of single women who endure unique challenges in the area of romance. Please keep in mind that educated Black women are not exclusively Black women with formal training. Included are all Black women that possess an unforgiving progressiveness toward their best life. You know who you are. And while some boy-meets-girl challenges transcend culture and economics, additional challenges face this demographic. So let us get to the real on what is going on.

Dexter R. Conner

Los Angeles, California
February, 2014

[E-Mail Correspondence]

Dear Dexter,

I am a 33-year-old Black woman from Asheville, NC. I'm 5'6", a shapely size 10, with an MBA. I attended an HBCU and now work in the corporate arena making a six-figure salary. I relocated to Atlanta for my job nine months ago and bought a condo in the mid-town area. I'm very disappointed with the fact that I've not met a nice eligible Black man to date. It seems that the guys I meet are players, gay, intimidated, married, or just unwilling to be in a monogamous relationship for any length of time. It is beginning to affect my self-esteem and I find myself depressed about the whole situation. My dream is simple—I want a nice man, preferably with a college degree, and definitely a decent job. It would be nice if he is fairly handsome too and a few inches taller than me. But I'm willing to compromise a bit if he's really nice. I'm a member of a mega-church here in town but it seems that the church men are no different. At times, I just want some attention from a male figure. I realize that sounds pitiful, but increasingly, I find myself needing validation from men. My father was in and out of my life growing up, so I think there is some anger that I have toward him too. I'm hoping you can offer some perspective on how I can feel whole again. I did read Steve Harvey's book but need something just a bit more specific to my situation. Thanks for any insight you can provide.

Sincerely,

Dawn

[E-Mail Correspondence]

Hi Dawn,

Thanks for reaching out. You are not alone. Many educated Black women express similar feelings. There is no quick answer or automatic remedy. But there are immediate ways you can gain strength and perspective on your current state. First of all, I am happy that you found a good church home. Renew your spirit of goodwill and confidence by reading the bible consistently and through prayer. Also, understand that feelings change and perspectives evolve. So don't do anything irrational due to temporary dissatisfaction. You know, like falling for a "scrub" because you are lonely. I look forward to helping you over the next few months to move your life forward. Your first assignment is to read my book. It is very inexpensive as an e-book so just download it. It is sure to broaden your perspective. After you complete it, e-mail me back. Tell me what you have learned and how it makes you feel. It is short, so read it this week so you can e-mail me back soon. You've got a bright future with exciting places to go and great men to meet!

Sincerely as we go,

Dexter R. Conner
drconner@faithindreams.com

CONTENTS

To be young, gifted, and Black
Relationship Dynamics for Educated Black Women

Hello to young, gifted, and educated Black women reading this letter. You are probably living the good life or something close to it. It may include a French titled bachelorette pad, a Chanel handbag, and an occupation well worth feeling proud. You may even be climbing the corporate ladder in Jimmy Choo stilettos. Kudos! I'm definitely impressed. But your achievements do not exempt you from possibly being unlucky in love. In fact, you may be a significant contributor to your romantic relationship challenges with Black men. Do not misunderstand me; I am not going to let Black men off the hook. But this particular letter will focus on you, the educated Black woman, as the star attraction. We often hear about the disappointment in Black men regarding their inability to commit or for their selection when it is made. And sure, some things are funky about Black men's approach to relationships. But please allow me to save those thoughts for another letter. For now, let's just peel back your onion.

Educated Black women honor the holy trinity, have made the grades, and are careful not to indulge premarital improprieties. Right? Your resumé is tight. But you feel disappointed, maybe even pissed-off at the selection of Black men, their credentials, manners, and choices pertaining to love and marriage. This dilemma plagues more than just Black women (Asian men have similar challenges). But I do believe that Black women are ostracized enough to explore new rules of engagement.

On the dating scene, many educated Black women are frustrated in dealing with the less polished Black male population. These Brothers balk at the non-traditional roles taking shape within new age relationships. Not as a conscious vice per say, but as a subconscious conditioning. Black people are usually traditional. And Black men are chicken-hearted about committing to serious relationships if they believe themselves to have monetary instability. Another antagonist is that there are a vast number of beautiful, available women. It becomes difficult for Black men to see value in settling down when there is such an open dating scene. It is understandable that these challenges can be discouraging to discerning educated Black women. But although looks can be deceiving, faith in God's ideals that sustain you for suitable companionship cannot. Remember, you are only looking for one good man to connect with; and he is looking for you. Only in God's timing can you find one another. Jesus Christ is an on-time God. Operate within God's purpose for your life. He will provide peace within and clarity to your interactions with men. Believe it and be prepared to receive it. *Trust in the Lord with all your heart and lean not on your own understanding. In all your ways submit to him, and he will make your paths* straight (Proverbs 3:5-6 NIV).

Stormy Weather

The lack of legitimate male suitors often creates stress for single women. But there is no need for educated Black women to feel that way. Men that are unwilling to romance you are a blessing in disguise. Many men will allow egotistical and underdeveloped elements of their personality to steer them away from women cultivated beyond their comfort zone. Educated Black women should be thankful for that. Life is short. There is no time to waste. Relationships with these men would create more problems than solutions toward your best life. Educated Black women are treasured by men cultivated beyond traditions of sexism. Black men that understand their own plight, career path, sexuality, and responsibilities are not just sitting on every street corner. But rest assured that they are scurrying around preparing for educated Black women. Are you paying close attention? These men come in various and sometimes unexpected forms. They may be wearing glasses with political contacts, have financial figures making cents, are legally blind offering vision for the future, and off shades of brown talking Black. Usually the man for you is much closer than you think. He may have even shown you interest. You may not have considered him for companionship due to trivial reasons. Be careful to not overlook a high character man that is really vying for your attention. That man is likely to show you a high level of value within a relationship.

Educated Black women must use the same meticulous eye offered on Louis Vuitton pursues in distinguishing a quality man from a fake. It is important to choose relationships wisely and not out of desperation. We will come back to that later. Beware of buying the tickets without seeing that game, going on dates without leaving the house, or opening your heart if he is not a cardiologist. Just kidding! All I am saying is, *let us not be weary in well doing: for at the proper time we will reap a harvest if we do not give up* (Galatians 6:9 NIV). Never question God's well intentions for you in romance. He is your heavenly father. All fathers want the very best for their daughters. Trust in him. Those duds that are wearing sunglasses but are shady, have money but are still broke, tall but are short sighted, think they are big-time but are small minded, and talk loud but are saying nothing can leave that smell of onion on you so foul that other men will not dare approach. Discernment is the key to unlocking life's blessings.

Pairless souls wander the earth in search of a companion. They search in places that are empty and pointless. The best place to look is right in front of you. Love is an intriguing thing. But searching for it will get you nowhere. Let it come to you. If you are patient enough and keep an open mind and heart, then love shall appear before you in its simplest form: another soul (Anonymous).

Educated Black women have specific relationship challenges even among the Black population. Their battle cry can vary due to the diversity of the Black experience. Many educated Black women do have a huge breath of steam to exhale about relationships, while others are just blowing smoke. But, let me be clear. Some educated Black women are happily married, earning a six-figure salary, and enjoying a nice family and home due to existing definitions. These women have been able to ascend within the current atmosphere. It could be because they have had advantages, worked hard, or are particularly blessed. Each situation is different (all are blessed). For instance, I know a very light-complexioned Black woman that has family ties to opportunities within academic and professional societies. These affiliations positioned her for easy access to academic and monetary achievement. In the dating arena she grapples moreso with the quality of applications from Black men that are pursuing Black women, versus none at all. She also seems to get a serious interracial pursuer from time to time. Her situation is just one story. And her story is not the norm. But it does showcase how the diversity of Black culture provides different experiences. The masses of the educated Black women I encounter have families that more recently gained opportunities at academic achievement. These educated Black women now rise within corporate sectors enjoying financial freedoms and titles never experienced in their families. The plights of educated Black women will always be unique to their existence. Is it likely that these women will respect their diversity by uniting to strengthen one another? I hope so. I will stay tuned to how things are going by watching reality television shows like *Housewives of Atlanta, Mary Mary, Married to Medicine, The Braxtons, and Love & Hip-Hop.*

The Game
Relationships are Competitive

An irony of the dating game is that the code that bonds women on national women's issues is lost when tending to matters of the heart. Relationship politics are tenacious. They are quite similar to the power politics of men. Self centered agendas take precedent. Some women plot, scheme, and compete tremendously for available and committed men. Society teaches women that the pickens are slim. Therefore rules of morality in engaging companionship are often out the window. It can feel like survival of the fittest. Women like Fantasia, LeAnn Rimes, Rielle Hunter, Angelina Jolie, or the Tiger Woods mistresses continuously up the ante on what is possible within the game. Especially as book deals, spot lights, and other financial incentives are awarded to these women. As the relationship game becomes more competitive, cosmetic enhancements are greatly tinkered with to gain attention from men. Black women spend 80% above the national average on cosmetics. The inner-self is sure to hemorrhage from every outward adjustment that does not attract a man. Even if it does, silicone compositions sag while spiritual connections endure. Psychological baggage and fear of karma from fake relationship tactics often creates insecure, devious, and complex women. Connections based on deception affects the ability to have a true relationship. The truth pertaining to who you are is the strongest foundation to attract a comparable man and build a sustainable relationship with him. Gain confidence in your god-given qualities and the sincere person you have worked to become. God rewards a mind aligned with positive thoughts. ...*Blessed are those who have not seen and yet have believed* (John 20:29 NIV). Believe in God. Believe in yourself. Believe that you are worthy of a positive relationship. Gradually you will become strengthened with positive and sustainable relationship qualities, and the ability to recognize those traits in others.

Educated Black women should always strive to be at their very best. Do not abandon the positive direction in which the Holy Spirit leads, in an attempt to appease an unsatisfactory man. Do not act out of desperation. If you do, you will quickly become unsatisfied. Because the authentic connection that comforts the soul will be absent. You will always be discontent within a relationship where there is no authentic connection. An authentic connection means being equally yoked in some basic ways. Here are a few basics. The man should be a Christian, should love you, want to provide for you, and be family minded.

It pays for educated Black women to look their best by having those legs cocoa buttered down to the high-heels. But we must acknowledge some deeper challenges facing the psyche of some Black women. For instance, some Black women gloat about being a descendent of Native Americans or another ethnicity. It is true that most African Americans are multi-racial. But it is often said with pride, or offered as a status symbol beyond simply claiming to be Black. What is interesting is that Native Americans and others usually have no interest in claiming them as relatives. It is equally unfortunate that Black culture often preserves and ideology that places higher value on physical traits that imply a diverse genealogy. Another example is how Chris Rock's copycat film *Good Hair* caused the film *My Nappy Roots* to have a really bad hair day. Not only did *Good Hair* reconfigure the substance of the real hair story, it attracted millions of Black women while *My Nappy Roots* has been reduced to short viewings in "kitchens" across the country.

Society's laws of attraction are learned and eventually ingrained within us. How the laws of attraction are defined among Black people is essential to the value placed on each other in relationships. Many Black women have struggled with how to outwit God in creating what they believe to be a beautiful new reality of themselves. In defining laws of attraction, Black women increasingly defer to hair extensions, hair textures, or physical features that contradict their God given beauty. Inner values are not usually kept there. And Black men value beauty by how it is defined by Black women. Educated Black mothers have an initial opportunity to influence their Black boys. Remember, the standard is being set for what future educated Black men value. So look at yourself. Are you helping your cause or hurting it?

Waiting to Exhale
Relationship Pressures Can Spiral Out Of Control

Years after college, single educated Black women begin losing their confidence in the dream of having an educated Black husband. Especially among educated Black women that have never experienced a good romantic relationship with an educated Black man. Educated Black women also begin to worry about their biological clocks, and the ability to have children. Relationship challenges become even more complex since proximity to new educated Black men becomes the issue. The routine of life makes it difficult to meet new quality men. Some educated Black women become jealous of those other women that easily meet men. Not the women that did not pursue traditional education or careers. An education and career is not nearly as relevant as companionship and family to most women as they get older. But rather groupie women that undercut what educated Black mother's teach as respectable relationship tactics with men. These groupies are ruthless, exist as sexual misfits, and often possess the latest artificial body enhancement. Their ability to attract the high rollers can be infuriating to educated Black women. Not only because the dream is for men to value an educated woman over his carnal desires, but because reality is that the dream is usually within a fantasy world. (Remember, these men are not for you. You need one that values an educated Black woman. Stay focused!) It may even be resented that she has a kid, his kid. Educated Black women usually desire children too and have no desire to share their man with an uncouth baby-momma. It may appear that the groupie has the good life, while an educated Black woman's life mirrors the television show *Being Mary Jane*. But groupies are not in healthy relationships with these men. They are also not building a life that ever attracts the type of love and fulfillment to be happy. An educated Black woman must know that groupies are never the competition. So stop rolling your eyes at those skanks. They are who they have chosen to be. And how those women are valued by men is in line with their lack of standards. They actually help by weeding out men that are not ready for a serious relationship with an educated Black woman. You need a man that is ready for a wife and that places value on what a virtuous Black woman brings to the table.

Some educated Black women do find a single educated Black man, while others refuse to compromise for what they feel is a lesser man. The relentless power of loneliness makes some educated Black women decide to settle for Mr. Right Now instead of Mr. Right. Mr. Right Now may already have a lady or simply be unacceptable. But low self-esteem and mental numbers games are used to justify the involvement. The hope is that her prodding will zap him into shape and creates a fulfilling relationship. Deeply rooted is the feeling that if she is chosen for marriage, even by this clown, it lifts a dreaded societal pressure. Maybe it does. Next may be a kid and voila, what a beautiful family! Whether the relationship works is of concern, but the desperate actions thus far have shown that a healthy relationship has fallen as the priority. There becomes a twisted solace in the statistics of most relationships ending in divorce. She knows her relationship is not built on sustainable qualities. But the truth is that she has misused her time and true emotions by being with this man. The relationship will not work. Even if the two individuals stay together in title, there will be no genuine connection. Let me explain why.

Expectations are always greater in marriage than when dating. An educated Black woman will resent Mr. Right Now's inability to represent what she feels her husband should be. She expects him to be educated, strong, loyal, caring, funny, and able to vacillate between the executive boardroom and the neighborhood. His shortcomings may be reality. But her continuously telling him of his inability to measure up will be devastating to the relationship. He may leave since there are available women that he believes would treat him well. Or, he may consider staying if there is a child involved. Either way, her emotional state will attribute his lack of abilities for their relationship woes. Usually this educated Black woman is comforted by single Sisters that tell her that she is the latest victim of the inadequacies of a Black man (Be careful of always talking to single people about your relationship problems). That is not necessarily true. Educated Black women must make strong choices from the start if they want to have a fruitful relationship. That includes prioritizing education, work, and dating choices with long term goals in mind. That long term vision helps keep a reasonable standard when considering a man worth spending precious time. Educated Black women that deal with men that are obvious duds are setting themselves up for major life problems. Do not be that woman. You will regret it.

Remember, this educated Black woman made a decision to deal with a man that is unable to lead her. This could actually make her not so educated after all. The decision is a huge problem since God placed man as leader of the family. How can a woman follow the leadership of a man she ultimately does not respect in that role? She cannot! But this educated Black woman decided to settle for this man. That secret is kept just beyond the wishing well in her consciousness. She wishes that he would turn into more. But each day she wakes up to the same dud. Married and with a child, the societal pressure is gone. She made it. The road to premonition will begin as this man proves in marriage to be exactly what he presented in dating. All close friends know of the relationship mismatch. Not just from the obvious discrepancies when seeing them together, but from the concerns she expresses in moments of truthful emotion. But everyone is an adult, at least age wise. Opinions on the matter from even close friends are careful, and sometimes silent. Reality is that this educated Black woman's relationship desires moved from being a God-centered pursuit to self-centered ambition.

Even mothers of educated Black women often push unreasonably for their daughters to get a husband. The mothers want grandkids like their friends and usually believe that their daughter's life will not be fulfilled without marriage on the resumé. Often mothers make the mistake of encouraging their daughters to accept a wedding ring regardless of some serious red flag's that may be apparent. This can be where much of the direct pressure is felt by educated Black women to get married. Daughters sometimes conform to the pressure by jumping into senseless marriages. There is no parachute that opens to save the relationship's swift spiral downward. The only saving grace for many educated Black women is that their formal education will continue to provide means to support themselves once the relationship fiasco is complete. But they also may be stuck paying alimony to their ex-husbands.

This may not be his dream either. I am speaking about the man in all of this. He might be working through apprehensions of his own. The thought of this may seem silly to his educated Black wife. Her feelings primarily will be based on her bank account versus his, which she keeps separate. She may feel that she has upgraded his life. That could be true, financially. But even financial matters serve as a tremendous obstacle in the relationship. The relationship now mirrors society in grappling with what it means for women to bring home the bacon, instead of cooking it. Black relationships also like to include Biblical perspectives, though they are not followed with any more regularity than other relationships. Without a Godly influence, relationship challenges cannot be resolved. They can be bandaged for a time, but the problems will eventually resurface. Usually it is in a more devastating manner than if the situation had been nipped in the bud from the beginning. It is very important for educated Black women to connect in a genuine relationship with a God-fearing man. Not only to minimize the number of obstacles within the relationship, but to have the highest form of authority available to regulate the multitude of challenges that will occur.

This man's American dream played it vice versa. He was making the big dough (money) in the relationship and therefore running the show. That may be her dream too. For that reason, her emotion on their reality places her as driven, focused, and capable while him as not so much. She is reminded of Brothers who are "on her level" in *Ebony*, *Jet*, and *Black Enterprise* magazine. Or this educated Black woman marvels when watching Black professional athletes. Athletes meet her monetary, glamorous, and fantasy physical dimensions. Not to mention imagining the ego boost of having been chosen by a man who has his choice of women. She views her actual man as a compromise. But she often forgets that he is the one she settled for. Perspective that her man offers pertaining to Black women having it a bit easier in Corporate America than Black men is heard by her as an excuse. It could be partly an excuse coming from him. But again, she should have assessed his potential in the dating process. He envisioned his wife to have different attributes too. She was to look more like the video vixens he grew up seeing in hip-hop videos. Or with physical qualities similar to the women those athletes marveled at are able to marry. But, he is also responsible for his shortcomings in relation to his pipe dream. And like Walter Lee Younger *(A Raisin in the Sun)* in the answer to *What happens to a Dream Deferred*, he is plagued with insecurity, inadequacy, and a woman who is taught to respect men that are much of what he is not. He too settled, instead of developing himself emotionally, educationally, and spiritually in a manner that would help him identify and strengthen a positive romantic relationship. It is hard to clean-up marriages that begin as one big mess. The best solution is to keep your hands clean from the jump. Do not get caught up in a relationship that you know is not a Godsend.

Many of the handsome Black men with swagger educated Black women want as an option are starring on the documentary television show *America's Hardest Prisons.* If released, they are facing tremendous odds of not getting sustainable employment and going back to prison. The formally educated Black men, instead of marrying out of college, chose going to graduate school and now believe themselves a prize. They are correct. It is interesting because many were geeks that could not get a date a few years prior. But their focus on education has turned the tables. These men are now in good careers. It is finally their time to shine. Some become cocky and hold off on any relationship commitment. Others are ready to begin a family. These are men that educated Black women should get to know. I am not suggesting just any man with an advanced degree. Make sure you are attracted to him and that he is Godly. But these men have demonstrated that they possess some ambition. It is also ideal if the man is a referral from a mutual contact that can vouch for his character. But do not let that hold you back from gradually getting to know a gentleman with good credentials. Also educated Black women should consider blue-collar Brothers that are handling their business. Be open. Because left in society are some good men that are in committed marriages. Stay away. There are married men that are not committed to their relationship. Stay away. Also, there are momma's boys. The momma's boys are usually spoiled and underdeveloped victims of the absence of strong fathers. These men want women to do everything for them. Stay Away. And every since The Oprah Winfrey Show's 2004 episode titled *A Secret World of Sex: Living on the 'Down Low'* aired, underground homosexual Brothers remain polarized in Black women's consciousness (E. Lynn Harris must be acknowledged for making this phenomenon mainstream with his book *Invisible Life*). Stay away. You cannot make a gay man straight. All of this adds to perceptions regarding the unavailability of Black men for relationships. It is true that there are not as many educated Black men as Black women would like available. But you are only looking for one good man. An educated Black woman should focus on her own preparation toward a happy relationship. That is what is in your control. That is done by staying positive about life and love, and continuously bettering yourself. ...*faith by itself, if it is not accompanied by action, is dead* (James 2:17). Spring into action, and have faith that God will too.

The Infamous
Political Relationships Shaping the Neighborhood

It can seem dreamy what life may have been like had all Black Africans re-boarded *The Amistad*. But, I am not sure that it would have been best to sail back to Africa. There are so many struggles there too. Plus, some powerful Black Africans were the very reason so many people were taken away in slave ships in the first place. How else would White men consistently dock huge ships, and manage to carry off 20 million Black men, women, and children. Anyway, *Roots* would have been fiction, *To Kill a Mockingbird* a crime, *Watermelon Man* about a farmer, *Sweet Back's Bad Assss Song* off pitch, and *Before They Die* a bucket list comedy. Reality however has issued the content of these films with a voice adverse to such a dream. Although each film's nightmare scenario provides a relevant commentary, the central themes are common within the African American experience—struggle. It has become such the norm that lives of danger and poverty have been transformed into the criteria of authenticity ("being real") in many Black neighborhoods. This foolish mentality sustains the hope of hopelessness recognized on Martin Luther King Boulevards around the country.

In short, it characterizes extreme injustices in a manner that lightens the burden on a flawed system. This system attempts every justification imaginable to place responsibility of opportunity and success solely on each individual. It furthers the cold war within American politics that arrogantly insinuates that the majority of Black people must prefer to engage lack instead of well paved streets, safe communities, supermarkets with fresh produce, bountiful park space, and long healthy lives. The truth is that legislation that supports the privileged shifting significant amounts of sustainable resources to uplift the disenfranchised seldom happen. American history unfortunately showcases threats of violence, riots, or financial boycott as the most successful manner for disenfranchised individuals to *Lift Every Voice and Sing*. Many Black people are eternally muted during the various struggles for survival. Many others are stuck in lives of dreams deferred. The song *2nd Childhood* by Nas poetically articulates the cycle of going nowhere experienced too often within our communities.

The overwhelming reality is that fertilizer for greener pastures is hidden from families that have been subjected to generations of Third World conditions in America. Basketball *Hoop Dreams* of one in a million become almost greater odds then Black and Brown school age kids rising from dilapidated, violent, overcrowded, and understaffed schools. Many of these schools are similar to Eastside High School in the film *Lean on Me*. The chances of these twenty seven million kids ever living in neighborhoods with the suffix Hills, Lake, Estates, or Beach is very unlikely. However, since men are visual and will enact the prince charming fairytale of rescuing a damsel in distress, around-the-way Boricua looking women have had the greatest opportunities to cuddle up to money. For most others, the access into financial ranks of the American Dream is terribly limited. We all know a few success stories. But it is pathetic how vernacular, area code, skin color, and accents foreign to the majority can limit minority children to living vicariously through rap videos. Many White kids are also limited, and love rap videos. But White Privilege can better their chances at living in a safe neighborhood and getting a job.

Recent data insist that there have been no sustainable systems to rectify the disparities in Black communities. This is true particularly as it pertains to wealth and financial earnings. The census defines "Households" as all people occupying a housing unit regardless of relationship. With that expansive definition only 1.5 of the 15 million Black households have an income of $100,000 or more. Per capita income among all Blacks is $18,406. This lack of financial resources adds to the disjointedness of Black families. It also cripples the ability for Black men to gain confidence or respect from Black women as husbands, fathers, and family men. Today represents the most desperate point for Black progress. The inability to acquire, merge, then focus resources makes the future bleak. Even relevant numbers of The Talented 10th are following the wrong pioneers. Instead of King, X, Belafonte, Parks, and Angelou they use the ideology of America's pioneers that valued individual preservation, accomplishments, and money as most significant. Unfortunately there are now Clarence Thomases at every turn trying to make a deal with the devil.

Another commonality of the films initially mentioned in this section is that they are written by men. Men are worthy of writing their share of stories. It becomes discriminatory when they write most of them. It precludes the authenticity of women's experiences. Black women's perspectives particularly have all but completely been ignored in film and other aspects of life. Sure, the film *The*

Help offered a tale of triumph and camaraderie among Black women. Even that fictionally conceived story was written by a female White writer and directed by a White man. Was it a good story? Sure. But Black women have specific experiences that can only authentically be told by them. At the very least they should be afforded that platform. Whether films, books, academia, television, or other mass communications, their voices should be heard, felt, respected, and considered in every decision made in society. Especially if society expects to advance to the point of valuing what's communally best. Black women could speak to the essence of our possibilities and setbacks, our history and future, the school systems and our homes, our families and relationships. How? Black women have been forced to experience it all, digest it all, and mostly internalize their perspectives and solutions. As a group they have had no opportunity to be arrogant because their existence has never even attained proper value. Despite this positioning Black women have used creativity and intelligence to become sensational. Having withstood the abuse of men from all colors and no real alliance with their White female counterpart, they keep on keeping on. Black women mother children that are not their own and serve as fathers for those that leave. They were used as cooks and cleaning for White women that hated them and bodies for White men they hated. They were forced to accept the White man's burden, lighten the Black man's, and forget about their own. Expected to teach their people reading, writing, and arithmetic, and to stay quiet about molestation, abuse and other crazy…stuff. And most indignant is that they have been expected to accept these things without any expectation of their own. Black women as a group have never gotten their due. But although they continue to endure the prejudices of color and gender politics, there are glimpses of providence all about. One extremely impressive group among them are the educated Black women, at least most of them. Next will be my thoughts on one educated Black woman in particular and how best educated Black women can push forward.

Obama: Forward
Relationship Fantasies of an Educated Black Woman

For me, watching Michelle Obama demands much more than an arousing applause. It was captivating to watch her grand entrance as a speaker at the 2012 Democratic National Convention. My focus fell to the fitted reddish dress on her sultry physique, the scratchy symbolism presented by her colorful manicure, and the five-inch heels that emboldened her calves. The standing ovation that she received upon taking the podium provided just enough time to transition my thoughts into matters more conventional. But the laws of nature reminded me that I too was just a man—simple. It became fantasy that I had known Mrs. Obama personally. But in a *Me and Mrs. Jones* type manner similar to what Billy Paul sang about.

I could smell the pastries from our inconspicuous upstairs seating at Café Verles in Paris. This is where months of intimate meetings endured. We purposely ignored the seasons changing in her life, until the need to move forward became overwhelming. She explained, only to prolong our final conversation, what the world had recognized two Democratic National Conventions prior. Her lanky, unknown, Illinois senator could change the country. The obligations she had to that change became much to demanding to continue our scheduled rendezvous. Gaps of silence now lingered without the laughter or bashful eye-contact usual when we were together. The feelings of blissful moments slipping away caused my desperate attempt. I decided to question her ambition. It was done by reminding her of the politics of years past that should relegate her optimism for change. It was a despicable angle for my selfish motives. And ridiculous enough to ease her decision that what we had was over. She abruptly grabbed her Tod's hobo bag, Prada sunglasses, and stood upon red bottom heels. She then slowed down a bit and just looked at me for a few moments. There was nothing more to say. But her sly smile gave insight into her thoughts. Not only had she enjoyed my company, she was going to miss it. Regardless, in educated Black woman fashion, she ended things by saying it was time for her to move forward from me, but for me. She was right.

I finally snapped out of the daydream. Then snickered at how the imagination can work in moments of salacious intrigue. Now focused in reality, I noticed Mrs. Obama's perfectly etched cocoa brown arms. My gaze eased up past her elongated neck to her gleaming white teeth. They seemed to glimmer every millisecond through the smooth glossiness of her lips. One final thought came about before it dawned on me that she was speaking. I am uncertain of how my ears had not been turned up considering the heightened volume of the television. She was almost done when I exhaled, hearing just seconds of her speech. There was an uncomfortable feeling that eyes had been observing me for an undisclosed amount of real-time. My mother-in-law at some point had entered the living room and sat beyond my peripheral vision. I did not think I had embarrassed myself, but had been in la-la land to a point that left me exhausted and now insecure. Many seconds passed before she facetiously offered the obvious question of the moment. "So how was Michelle Obama?"

Who could not be impressed with this First Lady of the United States, Michelle LaVaughn Robinson Obama? She had risen from the meager beginnings of the south-side of Chicago. And earned her way into Princeton where her thesis was titled *Princeton Educated Blacks and the Black Community.* Her knowledge of self was evident as she mentioned the discrimination within the fabric of her experiences at this Ivy League institution. She explained how her color seemed the leading factor in her interactions, regardless of how liberal many professors claimed to be. It is hard to know if the handcuffs of this analysis are stronger than that of her gender in modern society. But rest assured that educated Black women are often reminded of discrimination surrounding both. Mrs. Obama went on beyond Princeton to graduate from what many Americans consider the most prestigious law school in the world.

Enter stage left to the law firm, a skinny male mentee assigned to Michelle from her Harvard Law School alma mater. A few years older than her, he had a broken down car and lacked swag. His character struggled with identity problems stemming from the interracial union of his parents. But the fact that he wanted to be 'down' wasn't ostentatiously stereotypical. His big ears were rather cute. Plus he was naturally funny. After his several failed attempts, Michelle chose the film *Do the Right Thing* and blessed this Hawaiian native with their first date. She planned for the Spike Lee Joint to truly check his soul. It was necessary to see if he could represent her correctly around Chi-Town, her home town, and where he wanted to serve as a community organizer.

As he crept up in his rusted old jalopy he smiled with nervous anticipation of her reaction. "Chill" she said, as his insecurities with the 69 Camaro made him ramble on about it. Michelle was repin Black America's south-side of Chicago, where life had routinely included adversity. This car thing meant nothing. For good measure she added "It's not about the car as much as it is the driver…can you drive?" He was thrilled by her question, and began to clear his throat as if he could sing. In his best Jon Bon Jovi impersonation, he closed his eyes, and began to sing the hang on tight portion of *Born To Be My Baby*. Yes, this cat was corny. Michelle stayed completely silent until he opened his eyes. Then laughed to afford him the full shame he deserved. But in good conscious to not completely demoralize him, she landed a playful stinger, knuckles first, into his arm. "Can we please go to the movie?" she asked. He smiled. She had given him enough for his confidence. And her sixth sense predicted that she would be able to polish him up enough. Of course on a later date he proposed. She accepted, and became Mrs. Michelle Obama. She then gave him Chi-town's respect, beautiful children, and the family he longed for. Now it was almost time for the miracle.

Years passed, and Mrs. Obama endured the strain of primary caretaker of the kids, supporter of her husband's incredulous dreams, and worked as a professional lawyer. Now she was at the podium, center stage. Mrs. Obama had reached the pinnacle of her good decisions in moving forward. She stood in a position that no other Black woman had before as FLOTUS (First Lady of the United States). Despite the odds, the naysayers and the hardships, she had succeeded beyond where even modern era sensibilities encourage educated Black women to dream. No detail of the moment was without significance. The simple fact that Mrs. Obama was an educated Black woman married to a Black man of such prominence is unique. White chicks have customarily eased into the picture upon the beginning of royalty dollars. That fact was confirmed for Mrs. Obama by watching her own athletic and Ivy League educated big brother. He had divorced his Black wife and chosen a woman more the style. But this was Mrs. Obama's time, her life, and her legacy. She represented her family, her man, her people, and herself like an absolute queen.

The juxtaposition of the moment was not that Mrs. Obama was at the Democratic National Convention. But that with her credentials, she was not there to accept the nomination. Instead, her job was to rouse the crowd. And articulate in eloquent terms that if the President was good enough for her, he was damn sure good enough for us (That is what I later found out. Remember, I missed most of it). Her husband, Barack Obama, was the main attraction. Mrs. Obama served as his not so secret, secret weapon. The moment for African Americans served as one of the most proud moments experienced in the New World. For real, 'Fa Sho' Black people to be voted by America's majority White folks into the White House, despite their credentials, seemed about as likely as George W. Bush being voted President of the Nation of Islam.

Reality was that attitudes had only partly yielded change. It remained inconceivable for our current society to have yielded Mrs. Obama serious consideration or its derivative by the Electoral College. Although it is unknown if she would have wanted consideration for such responsibilities,

the point is that it remains far enough beyond
conceivability that even rhetoric opposing this educated
Black woman for the position has been unnecessary. We
know females that have gotten those opportunities. None
of them measure up to Mrs. Obama. But Mrs. Obama is
not White and privileged (Hillary Clinton), did not check
for Russia from Alaska (Sarah Palin), and would never
state that Hurricane Katrina was not a racial issue like
Condi did. This made her political options more limited in
our current society. However, God is alive and well. And
we all were able to witness the grace of God almighty. He
can show up and show out as he chooses. Mrs. Obama's
substance and enduring qualities prepared her to receive a
special blessing. That blessing led her to the occupancy of
a fifty-five thousand square foot mansion that in name and
color embodied the history of its preferred residents. Her
plight in arriving at this moment could rival any other in
history.

The hype around her being should be made more
considerable and led by the Black female constituency. I
am not suggesting in any fashion that causes Mrs. Obama
static. It could be through articles and forums, news papers
and term papers, books and radio shows, beauty shops and
nail salons. Educated Black women will have had a total of
eight years to lead the charge in creating new value for
Michelle Obama types (educated Black women). The
fierce urgency is in this moment. Let us not forget, Mrs.
Obama's knowledge, strength, and character helped back
dirty suckas up off her man. Her ties to the Black
community legitimized him for Black America. The
embrace of Mrs. Obama served as the most essential
resource in positioning Barack Obama to enter and sustain
the office of President of the United States of America. I

understand that more Brothers need to recognize that fact. But I am trying to make a different point here. If this opportunity is squandered, Black women will remain underappreciated. And whether due to intentional prejudices or the systematic types, the marvelous women in which an international icon like Mrs. Obama represents in romance, intellect, motherhood, and color will not have received new levels of value.

POTUS

Now, let me give props where they are obviously due. Barack Obama is the man! He is an educated Black man. He is no longer that skinny little confused dude. He is now a six-foot-two, basketball playing, White House living, Columbia University (undergraduate) and Harvard Law School graduating, beer drinking, former gunga smoking, charismatic, debonair, President of the Free World. He reps Chicago, listens to rap music, gives Jay Z and Beyoncé White House clearance, writes books, sings Al Green songs, provides glowing remarks of his wife at every turn, and is adored by his children. He comes across as a man we all knew, wanted to know, or aspired to be like. President Obama has been blessed by God, worked hard, and was smart enough to marry an educated Black woman! He therefore is living the dream and has become a miracle. No doubt. But all things considered, what does that make Mrs. Obama? She had most of the positive qualities listed before he did. I believe her to be an educated Black woman forced behind her time, whose existence however can move us forward.

I Know Why the Caged Bird Sings
Relationships Should Sound Good

A bird called the Song Sparrow sings crisply, clearly, and precisely. The Song Sparrow's sound is easily recognized by human ears because it sounds like no other. Although the Song Sparrow may know many songs, it has the tendency to repeat the same song many times. Song Sparrows learn these songs from their flock.

Like the Song Sparrow, educated Black women sing songs they have learned from others. The song sang regarding a healthy relationship with an educated Black man sounds like the most pessimistic song of all. The reason is simple. Single educated Black women are often surrounded by other single women. These single friends are often experts at telling relationship sob stories. While there may be some truth to them, remember that you are rarely privy to the man's perspective. Do not get me wrong. His version of the story is usually flawed too. There are normally three versions to a broken relationship story—her version, his version, and the truth. The truth falls somewhere in the middle and is always the most complex. But for now, let us examine the sob story educated Black women are hearing from their female friends.

Patterns often plague your friends' relationships (maybe your own). It could be that a particular friend always chooses thugs to date. Or, that she is quick to give up the cookie on the first night. It could be that she gravitates to controlling men due to her low self-esteem, or longs for a father figure because her father was not around. The list is endless. My point is this—your single friends are not always the victim. Stop believing that they are and allowing it to affect your attitude toward having a healthy relationship. There is no time for a victim mentality. Even those friends of yours that are not getting a date should stay open to trying *Something New*. Sitting around depressed or angry about not having an educated Black man to date is not pushing them any closer to one.

The bottom line is that another woman's negative words about relationships should not shape your reality. Words are extremely powerful. That includes the words that come out of your mouth and the words you consistently take into your consciousness. Your life will exemplify what you think and say. Make a choice to surround yourself with individuals that have positive relationship experiences. Those positive people can help push you in the right direction in terms of a healthy relationship, or at least show you how it is done. Educated Black women should always speak positivity into their lives. It is important to understand the incredible power of the tongue, and therefore use it for goodness. *The soothing tongue is a tree of life, but a perverse tongue crushes the spirit* (Proverbs 15:4 NIV). What song are you singing about educated Black men and having a healthy relationship? Sing a positive song and you just might speak it into existence. *Your beliefs become your thoughts, Your thoughts become your words, Your words become your actions, Your actions become your habits, Your habits become your values, Your values become your destiny* (Mahatma Gandhi).

Let me get specific about how Black people can begin singing beautiful songs together. Educated Black women often sing within a similar cycle as the Song Sparrow. That has been established. Brothers sing those sad songs too. The negative context speaks to the need for new song writers. The new song writers need to be educated Black men and educated Black women. Both genders have gotten off track. While Jill Scott's song *Love Rain Down On Me* stimulated both Black women and Black men to fantasize on such a fulfilling episode together, we should first recycle Angie Stone's *Brotha* lyrics or Black Star's *Brown Skin Lady*. Those songs establish appreciation for each other. Appreciation for each other is the first step toward developing healthy relationships.

How Black men and Black women sing about each other determines if we sing together. King, Dog, Chief, God, or whatever you prefer to be called Brother, next try grooving to Luther's *Can I Take You Out Tonight* or Common & Mary J's *Come Close to Me*. Those type songs provide some perspective on how to treat a Queen, when you are looking for romance. Queen, Bird, Lady, Dime, Sister, try humming Anita Baker's *Sweet Love* or *If I ain't got You* by Alicia Keyes throughout the day. The Brothers will appreciate it. Educated Black women and educated Black men believe themselves deserving of a beautiful duet. My point is that preparation for the life ballad is vital. When the music does fade into the lyrics of *Spend My Life With You*, it should caress your ears with a comfortable expectancy. *Sing to the Lord a New Song...* (Psalm 98:1) The Lord will hear you, and you will be blessed.

The rest of this chapter will be in plain English. I am done with the voice lessons. An educated Black woman should make the choice to speak goodness into her life. That does not mean she may not have some unfortunate relationship experiences. Life is no crystal stair. But an educated Black woman should always push forward with faith that a Godly man is around the corner waiting. And since a Godly man is what an educated Black woman wants, then that is what she is to prepare for. Singing beautifully will allow her to attract a man also singing a great song (I could not resist this last song analogy).

It is important to hear from successful relationships. But know that each relationship must find its own footing. Couples in the dating process must be honest on if they can make each other happy. If that is not possible, it is okay. That particular man is not the Godsend you hoped he was. In that situation, do not keep holding on to him. An educated Black woman will save herself from the additional drama if there is not the right connection by moving on. Trust me ladies, this is how an educated Black woman keeps from singing *Another Sad Love Song*. Fair enough? On the other hand, let's say the relationship is going well. It is crucial beforehand and after couples get married, that examples of healthy relationships are examined. Investigative discussions with well established couples can strengthen your understanding of the components that help sustain a relationship. Seek wise counsel. It is probable that you, your hubby, or neither of you were raised in the type of family you are now trying to create. Again, seek wise counsel. It may be difficult for you to engage great couples for mentorship since usually those that are great remain so because of the private, mature, and discretionary way in which they handle their relationship. Remember to be diligent and humble in approaching these couples. *Ask and it will be given to you; seek and you will find; knock and the door will be opened to you* (Matthew 7:7 NIV).

With good relationships it is natural to want to share the happenings. Be careful. Relationship envy can breed

success even among the closest of friends. Be conscious of
how a change in your Facebook status affects those around
you. Not everyone is a hater, but many good relationships
and marriages are poisoned by so called friends, family,
and others secretly jealous. It is necessary to remain
vigilant, realistic, and smart when evaluating advice or
sharing intimate details of your relationship.

I Am A Man! (For Men)
Relationship of the Black Man as Head of the Family

"Why don't you go back to Africa," was what this corn-fed,
White, teenage boy said. It was in a manner almost cynical
enough to mistake his request as an actual question. As the
stereotypical Hee-Haw pickup truck rolled slowly past our
home, I discontinued my yard chores and eased inside. I
can still see his paleface standing in the bed of that truck
smiling at me. The truth is that I was somewhat affected by
his insult. But I did not want that part known to my parents
who had been Black teenagers back in *The Sixties*. My
parents had prepped me for such bigotry, although it had
been two decades since integration laws had been passed.
That is when dark brown Black kids were allowed to be
raised in small towns where houses with antebellum
architecture had been sites of Confederate hospitals and
The Underground Railroad. Anyway, those struggles were
all history. Things were supposed to be different for me as
a nine-year-old Black boy.

Reality was that we were on an island in this east
Tennessee community. But it remained mild and breezy
compared to the impact Reaganomics was having where
our church and Black friends lived across town. I knew all
of this. Why then I felt obligated to tell my mother of the

racist comment must have stemmed from parental programming years before I can remember. I did the right thing and reported to her the interaction, nonchalantly though, cool like. I detected that she felt a familiar weight regarding the situation. It then dawned on me that she was raised in the Black Belt region of Alabama country. Unfortunately for her, she was tremendous at charades and in turn thousands of roles away from Academy Award consideration for acting. Despite her continuous attempts, her lines stammered out without the casualness I had displayed. Instead her maternal emotions oozed freely, easily upstaging the role she preferred to play.

By the time she had clarity on every detail, my father entered right on cue to join us in the kitchen. His demeanor was casual and movements like mine. All discomfort stopped following my mother's slightly dramatic rendition of my story. My father's body became sturdy, his eyes only in moments such as these particularly steady. Polished metal teeth from his Black fist afro-pick raked through his hair just seconds before he shoved it three-fourths of the way into his back pocket. He balked to caress his goatee which ensured time enough to digest the information. He too seemed to have been here before. And he knew our family would rally behind his direction. My father was our leader. Although he looked glaringly similar to Eldridge Cleaver on the cover of *Soul on Ice*, neither that name nor the book had yet crossed my consciousness. What happened next was inevitable of only great Black fathers. These are educated Black men that have acquired the discernment necessary to lead families, despite the intricate challenges dissected for us in the documentary film *500 Years Later*.

To my dissatisfaction this particular assailant would quickly become only symbolism for the idiots awaiting me in life. As I listened intently to my father, it was clear that such indiscretions were nothing necessarily unexpected. Also expected was my ability to navigate such incidents in a manner honorable of myself. I concluded that there were moments for various tactics old and new which all could be inflicted upon proper timing. Most importantly, my father would use this opportunity to serve as a barometer for his paternal grade in equipping his second son. Understanding that he must assess without prejudice to properly serve as jury, he also took on the roles of bailiff and judge presiding over this minor incident. His power was tremendous as it had always been. His words would greatly shape my approach and the emotional state of my mother, who lingered around as if she enjoyed housework.

My father was present for me physically and emotionally. He was there for us, the family. I have learned that being physically and emotionally present have equal importance. His presence brought security, vision, and a future. He knew me to express emotions a bit more than my brother and sister and even encouraged me when I decided to take my skills to Hollywood years later. We quickly found out that my acting bug was largely inherited from my mother.

The father should be the leader of the family. His headship is not always distinguished by income or physical abilities. To lead his family is a God given assignment. A God fearing father's relationship with God offers provision for his family. Some educated Black women have challenges with this setup. It is usually because they did not grow up with a strong father or are dealing with some self-centered knuckleheads that they do not respect in that role. Anyway,

God has made his decision on the matter. And people are a blessing when they honor the Word. The family starts within a father's loins and takes on an uncanny void without him. His value is incredible, and his presence for Black women, his children, and the community should be encouraged, applauded, and expected! Black men's inability to operate at expected levels in romance, fatherhood, or finances can cause them tremendous insecurity. Some fathers then neglect their responsibility. The affect of a father being alive and not present within his ordained responsibility is uniquely felt throughout society. Black men stand up! It is time to regroup and reposition as men, husbands, and fathers due respect from the children, families, and communities that we create.

The world is at war because its constituent states are improperly governed; these are improperly governed because no amount of legislation can take the place of the natural social order provided by the family; the family is in disorder, and fails to provide this natural social order, because men forget that they cannot regulate their families if they do not regulate themselves; they fail to regulate themselves because they have not rectified their hearts. They have not cleansed their own souls of disorderly desires; their hearts are not rectified because their thinking is insincere—their thinking is insincere because they let their wishes discolor the facts and determine their conclusions, instead of seeking to extend their knowledge to the utmost by impartially investigating the nature of things. Let men seek impartial knowledge, and their thinking will become sincere—let their own selves be regulated, and their families will automatically be regulated—not by virtuous sermonizing or passionate punishments, but by the silent power of example itself (Confucius | Our Oriental Heritage, 1935).

ProActiv Solution
Preparing for Relationship Success

The Proactiv commercials are constant. Their products must be tremendously successful to afford the advertising space and celebrity clientele featured on the commercials. I clicked on their website for a closer look. Within seconds Proactiv lived up to its name by providing a live chat box in the middle of the screen to address any questions I might have. The text read "How can I help you today?" I responded, "What is your favorite color?" to see if there really was a live person available. "Pink" was the response. After relevant correspondence on the product I finally replied, "I'm not sold on the products yet but thanks anyway." The rebuttal came within seconds. "You're not willing to be proactive in making your situation clear?" "Yeah, but I'm not ready yet." "That's fine. Then your situation will remain the same or get worse." My reckless response to her snide but true comment gratefully was expressed only in my mind. I was done typing to her. But I did scan over to the product offerings listed on the web-page. The title read *Introducing the new Proactiv. Your Answer: 3 Easy Steps, 24/7 Support*. Below three cleansers where shown with explanations of their abilities. The first was Renew: which features small micro-crystal benzoyl peroxide, designed to quickly penetrate pores to start killing acne-causing bacteria on contact. The next, Revitalize: the refreshing, alcohol free toner helps remove impurities and excess oils so your skin looks and feels clean, soft, and refreshed-not tight and dried out. The last, Repair: which gets deep into clogged pores faster but is designed to be gentler on the skin. It is an oil-free formula that is safe for your entire face.

Before clicking off the website, I pondered the merit of this cleansing method. Not for clogged pores but moreso for the poor mindset and care for ourselves that leads to emotional and physical insecurities. It is imperative to feel whole, and good about self and future. To Renew our spirit and perspective should be ongoing. To Revitalize our feelings, looks, and attitude are imperative. To Repair our hurts and emotions from past troubles is essential. Sure, there are rainy seasons we all go through, but it is nice to attempt a continuous cleansing of impurities as part of our daily regimen—body, mind, and soul. This routine is what provides a 24/7 support system within career, spirituality, and love.

The bottom line is that educated Black women are prayerful that the gentleman that steps to them will have himself together. Truthfully, it is an expectation, and rightfully so. What is he to expect from you mentally, physically, spiritually, and socially. People will attract what they are. So be what you want to attract! Otherwise, be quiet when continuously getting what you have been putting out for. I respect that you work hard and that time is at a premium. And we have all been meaning to get back to bible school or to the gym. But reality is that you have as much time as everyone else, and must allocate a portion of it to the development of self if you are to attract a top notch man. Time is fleeting. How and with whom you spend it with or without is important to your well being. I have a quote by Leonardo da Vinci on my desk that reads "I have been impressed with the urgency of doing. Knowing is not enough; we must apply. Being willing is not enough; we must do." What have you done to take your situation to the next level? Be proactive. And, like Proactiv, you are marketing yourself and should possess the necessary ingredients to be prepared to indulge men that are serious about a clear, smooth, and appealing future.

Before I clicked off the website I noticed at the bottom of the page the Proactiv Wedding Kit. It contained Proactiv Renewing Cleanser, Proactiv Revitalizing Toner, Repairing Treatment, Deep Cleansing Wash, Refining Mask, Green Tea Moisturizer, Travel Kit, Oil Blotter Sheets and Advanced Blemish Treatment. Nope, do not get cold feet about marriage now!

The Dilemma
Relationship Politics of Black

The December thirtieth evening was now a decade ago in Hotlanta. We chose a Catholic church on Central Avenue just a faint breeze from the Black owned restaurant that mirrored the flagship one in Harlem. It was cool being downtown but feeling uptown. The eatery has shut down since. But it was somewhat upscale with a lady's serenade echoing from the piano in a manner to establish a sophisticated ambiance with a down-home southern swang. "If you're here you're family" is how it felt, though the kitchen was sure to have enough grease, butter, and swine to send the usual Olive Garden patron into a diabetic coma. Ribs, chicken, and a delicious mystery meat were accompanied by due sides and long stem glasses of sugary drinks. The private room I reserved for this rehearsal dinner was transparent, which allowed views of general patrons that were also dressed in chic linens. Naturally they ogled at us due to our exclusive seating. And we naturally acted as if we were indigenous to the VIP life. I noticed comedian J. Anthony Brown at the bar who happened to be starring on the television show *Like Family* filmed at NBC in Los Angeles. I was working at that studio at the time and enjoyed frequenting the shows Craft Service table while watching the live tapings. At least that is the version of the story which convinced him to come in and make a celebrity guest appearance. I figured it would be a nice final stamp on the evening.

She had been the roommate of my bride-to-be. And an extremely relevant part of what we felt were intellectual discussions commonly enjoyed when my college cronies accompanied me to Atlanta to rap with and to these Spelmanites. Inevitably each discussion circled back to the nature of relationships and this moment too could not dodge it.

Camera flashes were going off as I stood at the front of the room behind our celebrity guest. Protocol required that next I would conclude the dinner with the cookie cutter announcements of appreciation to the wedding party. The former roommate casually approached, but expressed her observations quickly with no particular attitude to speak of. She said, "It's interesting that all the light skinned girls are here with a date and most of the rest of us aren't." I attempted the million dollar smile which the Crest White Strips had lied about before offering the obvious. "You're light and…you don't have a date." The statement was a bit risky, but the white strips had caused enough sparkle for the split second needed to ease my rebuttal. "And what about my lady, we're getting married tomorrow and she's with the man of the hour." She first offered only a poker face, no teeth. So mine apprehensively faded away. She countered with the slyness of smile offered in spades just before the dude with the joker wild takes it off his forehead and slams it to the table. "My features are too Negroid.

Your wife is really pretty and not particularly dark…you know that!" With eyebrows curled and lips pooched my eyes fell upon my suede loafers. My mind began to churn. I needed to think about all that she was implying. By the time I looked up the flashes had stopped, the celebrity was gone, and she had somehow floated back to her seat without notice. I quickly scanned the room and it was true that her observation had left me with complex questions to investigate of an intra-racial, cultural, and political nature. For all this time had I been progressively naïve, or a conditioned participant in some of the relationship politics around me? Had this woman been speaking as an educated Black woman? Was her analysis even worthy of my thoughts? Maybe she was just a woman who wanted a date and therefore being critical of others.

Whatever the color and features of my bride, I had been caught hook, line, and sinker. And although I knew that she was beautiful, I had never examined particularly why I felt that way. I got married the next day in front of 550 guests to a woman I felt was the most beautiful woman in the world. Fortunately true love leaves no space for an evaluation of societal politics. It rightfully serves as the guiding force in marriage that allows two individuals to operate as one team. The facts surrounding my commitment, shoes, celebrity guest, groomsmen, wife's roommate, and our lard cooked menu of delectables have potential to embody both problems and solutions within Black people's consciousness. What do you think?

Guess Who's Coming to Dinner
Interracial & Intra-racial Relationships

Kloe & Lamar, Ice Loves CoCo, Kendra, House of Joy, and *The Kardashians* on Reality TV. Dr. Christina Yang (Sandra Oh) with Dr. Preston Burke (Isaiah Washington) on *Grey's Anatomy*, Tom with Hellen Willis back in the day on the *The Jefferson's*, and Olivia Pope (Kerry Washington) and the President's *Scandal* on Primetime. I know you all have been watching that! Take Robin Thicke and Paula Patton, Kim and Kanye, or even the past Heidi Klum and Seal fanfare. The interracial scene is on and popping, especially in highly diverse metropolis around the country. In Hollywood circles it is particularly trendy to have liberal tendencies and it has even trickled down to the children. Hence Tom Cruise and Nicole Kidman, Charlize Theron, Michelle Pfiffer, Hugh Jackman, Angelina and Brad, Madonna, and Spielberg among the parents of Black adopted children, mostly from oversees. Whether it stems from the kindness of their hearts, is a political statement, or fashion accessory is unclear. But it is clearly *Different Strokes* for different folks. Despite the Arnold and Willis from Harlem or kids like *Webster* from Chicago not usually being considered for adoption, all children deserve a chance in life. True love from any person helps provide that chance. Some of these celebrities have even decided on rainbow tribes as Josephine Baker had. The democratic nature of Hollywood allows celebrities their benefits of the walk of fame which is to operate in an oasis where atypical behaviors can be openly indulged. Not only in ways where Studio 54 replicas offer pharmaceutical and sexual exposés, but in uniquely progressive thoughts and representations as well.

Let's cancel those dinner reservations for a moment and see who is bold enough to bring'em home to momma. I am talking about interracial romantic relationships. Black women dating interracially are much less polarized than their Black male counterparts. Although White men created a frigid relationship with Black women due to centuries of sexual abuse, many Black women have been open to expanding their romantic options by looking for love in all the White places too. Some seem to resort to this option while others are simply open to receive goodness, no matter the color. It is amazing how far this coupling has come. Tina Turner, Oprah Winfrey, Alfre Woodard, Iman, Whoopi, Diane Carrol, Josphine Baker, Zoe Saldona, Diana Ross, Kerry Washington, Dorothy Dandridge, Halle Berry, Naomi Campbell, Tatiana Ali, Garcelle Beauvais, Tamera Mowry, and Thandi Newton are only among Black celebrity ladies where White felt right, even if it was just for a time. Everyday Black women usually do not question their celebrity Sisters choices to date interracially. But they do sometimes cut their eyes at Black men that they feel may have pushed them to it.

The Gas Face

It has always tickled me when individuals say they do not see color when dating. How else would they know to make the statement? I understand the non-racist trajectory that they are attempting. Reality however is that colors are everywhere and no one is beyond having been provided some level of influence on what they mean and how best to engage them. White House-Black Market, Black Face-White Privilege, White Women-Black Boy, Black Balled-White Flight, White Horse-Black Mask, Black Magic-White Washed, Sleeping White-Talking Black, Fade to

Black-Acting White, White Christmas-Black Muslims, Black Berries-White Chocolate, White Supremacist-Black Power, Black Tie-White Collar, White Dress-Black Belt. These words may read as just inconsequential pairings or something much more. Either way, words have tremendous power. How they are framed, coupled, spoken, and created is understood within the paradox of our highly color coded society.

The first successful interracial rap group, 3rd Bass featured lily-White rapper MC Search. He avoided a white-lie when he gave us *The Gas Face* back in the 1990 hit single of the same name. Some of you will remember them from back in the day. To understand The Gas Face just think of the obvious face of contempt some Black women give a handsome and affluent Black man when he is coupled with a White woman. It is as if a fowl, thick, skunk type odor abruptly infringed within their nostrils. Do not act like you are not familiar with it. MC Search colorfully made his verse on The Gas Face a White on Black issue in his color coordinated flow. You should YouTube it if you do not remember, because it was tight. I intended to provide the lyrics of that second verse of the song here but music copyright issues are a trip. The green he made from this song kept him in the Black. So whether he was color struck, wore Cross Colours, or secretly listened to Color me Bad, his colorless skin created that unique platform from which he operated.

Make no mistake; color definitions sometimes caress the ego, while "colored" ones usually punch it. Often time perceptions regarding colors of people are simmering within America's quickly evolving melting pot. While the diversity of colors can provide a fantastic stew like aroma, it usually calls at least for seasonings from black pepper, brown sugar, red meat, mixed vegetables, and a side of crackers to transition tastelessness into a balanced meal for the mind, body, and soul. Intra-racial and interracial color politics are always delicate issues. I applaud the effort when it is genuine, but offer that the attempt to create a colorless society often discredits the uniqueness that a particular culture may offer.

Black women can be particularly brutal on educated Black men that date interracially. And nothing seems to discredit these men quicker among their race. Therefore some Black men have anxiety when dating interracially. Black men's participation in interracial relationships is often interpreted as them abandoning in mind, finances, and body the community that has paved the way. That is sometimes the case and in other instances it is not.

Helen (Mother): Don't even bring up that fool to me. Left me for some white woman.
Brian (Son): She's Hawaiian.
Helen: If she ain't Black, she white.
Brian: See, that's what I'm talking about mama! That's just ridiculous!
Helen: Fact of life
Brian: That's crazy. Latina women?
Helen: White woman with a taco.
Brian: Oh, so I just guess Asian women…
Helen: A white woman that don't speak no g*%#@mn English!

(The Brothers, 2001 Film)

The painter of all colorful portraits is Jesus Christ, with a mission of enhancing our society. "Red, brown, yellow, black, and white they are precious in his sight." It is interesting that children are quickly offered biblical nursery rhymes and boxes of crayons with a multitude of colors from which to create beautiful realities. What a drab life would be without the uniqueness of colors and their diversity. The option of loving who you choose seems a basic freedom. I mean, all color Christians praise Jesus that walked the earth Jewish. Often fear and jealousy from the outside world fuel intolerance. No culture is immune to having a staunch history of these qualities. The fact that these outlooks alienate the desires of the interracial couples involved in these relationships is what makes it ludicrous. What happened to integration, civil rights, or simply the songs *Opposites Attract* and *Ebony and Ivory*? At least the two songs seemed progress for our Christian nation and were number one hits, for God's sake! Amazing is that despite the naysayers within their families and communities, interracial couples are on the rise. It is admirable that they lean on *The Power of Love.* And instead of *Waiting on the World to Change,* decide to be the change they want to see in the world. Robert Deniro, George Lucas, Robert Ebert, Simon Cowell, Matthew McConaughey, Matt Damon, Bill Maher, Paul Wall, Ben Affleck, and Rupert Murdoch are among the White celebrity men that have chosen to date or marry interracially.

Guess Who's Coming to Dinner was a film about a thirty-six year old, handsome, Black, esteemed, male medical doctor named John Prentice. After only a few days he wants to marry a naïve White female nincompoop thirteen years his junior. He travels to her parent's home in San

Francisco to get permission for her hand in marriage from her quasi-liberal father who starts off livid about the idea. The Black male lead was played by the most significant Black Hollywood figure of all time, Sidney Poitier. His career would never be the same after the film's release. Although the movie became quite successful the *Blaxploitation* era on the horizon embraced a representation of Black men that shouted demands of White men instead of asking permission of them. Despite the White female lead opposite Poitier being Katherine Hepburn's niece and in her first role, her film career was also snubbed.

The movie was interesting, risqué, and banned down south. Its release in 1967 commemorated an interracially charged year in history. That year brought about the landmark civil rights decision of *Loving vs. Virginia*, which invalidated laws prohibiting interracial marriage. Also that year was the Pulitzer Prize for the fictional book *The Confessions of Nat Turner* written by a White man, depicting the Black folk-hero as lusting after a White woman. The book *Without Sanctuary: Lynching Photography in America* best chronicles through pictures of hanged Black men the tremendous fear, hatred, and injustice once created around the thoughts of Black men with White women. *The Scottsboro Boys*, *Rosewood*, *Emmitt Till*, Yusef Hawkins, the demise of *Black Wallstreet,* and The People of California vs. Orenthal James Simpson had much to do with the taboo of Black men and White women. Even a recent Cheerios commercial featuring an interracial family created online dissent strong enough to remind us that someone is still peeing in a lot of folks Cheerios. This remains a hot topic, which is why I have greatly bandied about until this point trying to figure out where to start.

Jungle Fever

I understand that you probably did not see *Guess Who's Coming to Dinner*. But surely you saw the Spike Lee Joint, *Jungle Fever*, starring the ladies love of the 1990's. If you have not seen it, you are some "slaw" (slaw: *(slang def)* terrible, not positive, out of the loop). The ladies love was not Cool James (L.L. Cool J), but Wesley Snipes. At least he was until he told of his preference of Asian Women. After that, many Black women thumbed their nose at him. They were his base audience, so his film career has not been the same since that time.

The film Jungle Fever starred Snipes as Flipper. Flipper is a Black, handsome, successful architect married to a very light complexioned Black Woman named Drew. However, he consummates a curious relationship with a cute White temp worker at his job named Angie from Bensonhurst's Little Italy. The backdrop is the Streets of 1990's New York City. Angie tells her friends who leak the information to her pops. Pops thoroughly beats her down then throws her up out of his house. Flipper tells his main homeboy, who tells his wife, who tells Drew. The jig is up. And Flipper comes home to his clothes, professional work, and all else catapulted from their 3rd floor window behind shouts of four letter explicits that I was hearing for the first time. Sista girl went loco on this Negro, and the whole community witnessed him getting kicked out. Drew leans on her friends for support. A conversation ensues led by Drew's dark skinned friend-girl that provides perspective on Black people's fascination through American history with romantic based color characterizations for women. They stem from *Light-Bright and damned Near White* to the exact opposite. The Black community is largely a victim of American history in this respect—literally. Within that spirit it is usually Black attitudes that uphold beauty preferences to light-bright, flo-and-blow women being in highest regard. That is why it is not necessarily surprising that this fascination has evolved to now include women from a multitude of other ethnicities. It may be disheartening for some people to accept the reality of this fact. But historical trends show that the day of interracial relationships being common among high earning Black men has been approaching.

Do any of you know what it's like not being thought of as attractive…I was always the darkest one in my class. All the guys ran after the light skin girls with long straight hair and that left me out – and it's that same kind of thinking that leaves us out when it comes to White women. Back in the day brothers would get sisters that look like you [referencing her light skin friend] – Today brothers going for the gusto, the real McCoy…White girls got it made.

(Jungle Fever, 1994 film)

Willie Lynch

A challenge facing dark skinned Black girls according to the documentary titled *Dark Girls* is their ability to feel beautiful. The reason is because we are in a society that promotes Eurocentric ideals of beauty. The ability to attract male suitors can have a large affect on if women feel beautiful. Dark skinned Black women do not usually receive proper affirmation of their beauty within our society. Many also feel that they are passed over for lighter skinned women for companionship. Attitudes surrounding the various colors and features of Black women were developed by White slave masters placing White women on a pedestal. White women were made the standard of beauty during that time. Slave masters also placed a higher value on light skinned Black women with features traditional of White women. It was common for White slave masters to bid-higher prices to purchase light skinned Black women that they personally wanted as sex slaves. That created an attitude that the closer a Black woman was to looking like a White woman, the more beautiful she was.

The slave era was the most debilitating time in American history to be a Black woman and considered beautiful. White male slave masters were often thinking below the belt. Light skinned children with characteristics traditional of White people were often born from the sexual abuse of Black women by these slave masters. These children often had greater chances of being privy to heralded in-house positions than the darker masses of slaves. But that became a curse to a Black woman if she was sent to a different plantation with a new master. She would quickly meet the same demeaning fate that her mother had endured.

Even the little child, who is accustomed to wait on her mistress and her children, will learn, before she is twelve years old why it is that her mistress hates such and such a one among the slaves. Perhaps the child's own mother is among those hated...Soon she will learn to tremble when she hears her master's footfall... If God has bestowed beauty upon her, it will prove her greatest curse. That which commands admiration in the white woman only hastens degradation of the female slave. I know that some are too much brutalized by slavery to feel the humiliation of their position; but many slaves feel it most acutely, and shrink from the memory of it. I cannot tell how much I suffered in the presence of these wrongs, nor how I am still pained by the retrospect. My master met me at every turn, reminding me that I belonged to him...The light heart which nature had given me became heavy with sad forebordings. The other slaves in master's house noticed the change. Many of them pitied me; but none dared to ask...They knew too well the guilty practices under the roof...to speak of them was an offense that never went unpunished.

I longed for someone to confide in... But Dr. Flint (slave master) swore he would kill me, if I was not as silent as the grave...

(Harriet Ann Jacobs | Incidents in the Life of a Slave Girl, 1861)

The slavery of Black people (1619-1865) lasted in America for almost one-hundred years longer than Black people have been legally free. The substantial time in slavery allowed the skin color and physical characteristics closest to White culture to become the leading standard for Black beauty, even among Black people. Those definitions are gradually changing in our society with beauty standards becoming more inclusive. But Black women characterized by White culture as the tragic mulatto in films like *Pinky, Imitation of Life,* or *Queen* are often women that are envied among Black women and sought by Black men. This is a challenge because it means the masses of Black women are not receiving proper validation. Every woman wants to feel beautiful. To not feel adequately valued as such by your own ethnicity is particularly devastating. The pathology of feeling inadequate is often passed down among Black women. This point may be best illustrated by Madam CJ Walker's incredible success with the hot comb. She became the first female self-made millionaire by providing a system to straighten Black women's hair. This exemplifies how necessary Black women felt it was to submit to White imagery. The fact that most Black women wear relaxers almost their entire lives means they feel some deep rooted challenges with their natural selves.

There is also a history within Black America of embracing the slave master's unforgiving class system that sometimes admonishes darker skinned individuals. Not only did the time Black people spent on slave plantations cause the rape of Black bodies, it fudged up the minds of many Black people. It is commonplace within Black American culture to lighten, straighten, and minimize classifications recognized as Negroid. Inevitably it means that Black people are often taught to feel elite when portions of their being are altered or inherited from western prejudices and unfulfilled if not. This is a particularly negative starting point when trying to empower beautiful Black girls. It offers negative perceptions of Black beauty if either they dislike their natural beauty, or love it for being different from traditional Black masses. We are obviously a multi-ethnic ethnicity, with an opportunity to embrace all of the variations that define Blackness.

Let me expand just a bit further with a few examples. I realize he is a man. But I will use the King of Pop as an example of how negative perceptions of self can take over. Michael Jackson was obviously very instrumental to Black progress. We all loved him as an entertainer. However, he always demonstrated a proclivity for Eurocentric standards of beauty. Jackson's hair, skin, lips, nose, wives, boys, and children all represented that which he was not, but obviously which he valued. This made him as a person seem *Off The Wall*, though as a performer he was a

Thriller. Another extreme example is chronicled in Elaine Brown's book *A Taste of Power*. She recalls in her neighborhood dark skinned female gangs that would cut the faces of random light skinned women that they hated because of their perceived advantage.

It is understandable why back in the day a person would rather go inside the big house over sweating it out in the outhouse. But, bigger does not always yield better. The intra-racial residual effect of this separate and not equal predicament that conditioned Blacks has made Willie Lynch in many ways significant as Dr. Martin Luther King, Jr. Class systems and beauty standards stemming from brown bags and flow-and-blow hair have limited the ability to appropriately appreciate our diversity within the race. Self love is applauded, but self centered or discriminatory love is not. Black people must believe that Black is beautiful. That belief is fundamental to progress. Even if the Willie Lynch letter was inconclusive, its ideology has proven true regarding the affect that slavery has had on Black people. Fear, distrust, and envy largely control the thought pattern of many Blacks. That is one big reason Black people have not progressed at an appropriate rate within American society. There is often a "crabs in a bucket" mentality.

... I caught the whiff of a dead slave hanging from a tree… You are not only losing valuable stock by hangings, you are having uprisings, slaves are running away, your crops are sometimes left in the fields too long for maximum profit… I have a full proof method for controlling your Black slaves. I guarantee every one of you that, if installed correctly, it will control the slaves for at least 300 years. I have outlined a number of differences among the slaves. And I

take these differences and make them bigger. I use fear, distrust and envy for control purposes...These methods have worked on my modest plantation in the West Indies and it will work throughout the South...On top of my list is "age,"...The second is "color" or shade. There is intelligence, size, sex, sizes of plantations, status on plantations, attitude of owners, whether the slaves live in the valley, on a hill, East, West, North, South, have fine hair, course hair, or is tall or short... I shall assure you that distrust is stronger than trust and envy stronger than adulation, respect or admiration. The Black slaves after receiving this indoctrination shall carry on and will become self-refueling and self-generating...Don't forget...you must use the dark skin slaves vs. the light skin slaves, and the light skin slaves vs. the dark skin slaves. You must use the female vs. the male, and the male vs. the female...But it is necessary that your slaves trust and depend on us...Gentlemen, these kits are your keys to control...

(Willie Lynch | Speech purportedly delivered in 1712, Virginia)

It is important that this section not overstate how Eurocentric standards of beauty have influenced Black culture. That is not always the case. Many Black men of prominence have chosen dark skinned Sisters. Denzel Washington, Sam Jackson, Barack Obama, Dewayne Wade, Courtney Vance, Eddie George, and P-Diddy are among celebrity men that have chosen dark skinned Black women for a lifetime commitment. The first Black super-model Naomi Sims, current super model Naomi Campbell, Tika Sumpter of the television series *The Haves and Have Nots*, and actress Gabrielle Union all have made or are making a living being viewed as beautiful, dark skinned

Black women that are sex symbols. One of my personal favorites was Keisha on the cult classic film *Belly*. These illustrations showcase that dark skinned Black women are desired. It is necessary however, for Black people to completely move from a color-struck slave mentality into the inclusiveness of our total selves. Every Black woman should feel beautiful in the skin and with the features God has provided her. God makes no mistakes. Black people are often mistaken for not realizing that fact and appreciating his diverse creations among us.

Dark skinned Black men do not suffer nearly as widely from color (or hair) politics in romance today. The main reasons are because male standards of attraction embody money and power as the most prominent. But even being comedic can win you a date. In the color politics of romantic allure, definitions have been transformed by entertainers such as Michael Jordan, Tyrese Gibson, Sidney Poitier, Morris Chestnut, Big Daddy Kane, Djimon Hounsou, Michael Vick, Tyson Beckford, Idris Elba, Leon, and other tall, dark, and handsome stars. Dark skin on a Black man is now often recognized as strong, manly, beautiful, and often sought for romance (It has not always been that way). On their female counterparts, it can more quickly be relegated to an exotic fantasy of a sexual rendezvous without commitment. It is not right. But with all the years of baggage, Black people as a group have not spearheaded the charge to completely go left.

Single White Female

"As far as I knew white women were never lonely, except in books. White men adored them, Black men desired them and Black women worked for them" (Maya Angelou). It is interesting that at least a few of Angelou's husband's were White. But, that fact is not particularly relevant to her point. Right? It is probably time for me to list Black celebrity men that have dated or married interracially as I did with White men and Black women earlier. But is that really necessary? The list would be particularly lengthy and therefore not accomplish much beyond what we already know. Since there would be nothing noteworthy accomplished, I will switch to thoughts of White women. White women are not usually considered in holistic terms in Black conversations about interracial relationships with Black men. At least not beyond the negative themes that sometimes even get projected onto light skinned Black women too. White women are often minimized to being gold diggers with insincere feelings. That is not always the case. Reality is that they too have cultural capital along with familial and social relationships that they are putting at risk. Many are now risking more than everybody in these interracial deals when weighing the inherited securities of staying within their ethnic group. White women, like all women, want a successful man. If it happens to be with a Black man, it is narrow-minded to think she should evade positive companionship for her life. Reality is that she had no more decision on her color (or the politics associated with it) than any of us. And any progressive minded person's goal is to live their best life despite societal prejudices.

Consider this, should White women believe that if a handsome and rich White man approached a Black woman, that she would not consider his proposal? Let's not forget when Robin Givens took Brad Pitt up on the offer. I understand that it is frustrating for Black women that feel as if another woman that has not paid her dues is constantly stealing luxury seats at the table. But Black women should be discerning in their reaction. Remember, what you are looking for is looking for you. Trust that. Just be sure that as the growing diversity of men riding by take a look, that the carpet matches the drapes and the bushes are trimmed. When a good man notices a fashionable, approachable, and interesting woman with a brick house, he will stop. Eventually, you will have no interest in guessing who's coming to dinner. Your time will be spent smelling long stemmed red roses and deciding which restaurant to indulge before enjoying a nice flick.

Silvie (For Men)
Appreciating Relationships with Women

It was a few weeks before the appreciation luncheon when an administrator at *USC Shoah Foundation: The Institute for Visual History and Education*, called me. She asked if I could pick up a lady on my way. The lady was also among the volunteers that were to be honored for service. We were not acquaintances, but had both been instrumental during the early years of the foundation's development. During that time we worked out of several trailers on Universal Studios' backlot just steps away from DreamWorks. The foundation had since moved to the University of Southern California and grown into its mission to be of service to the world. It was bitter-sweet that the foundation did not really need our efforts anymore.

But nice that they kept us in the loop and made us feel relevant.

I agreed to pick up the lady on my way to the luncheon. The administrator from the USC Shoah Foundation provided me her necessary contact information. I spoke pleasantly with the lady about a week prior to the event, and called before leaving on the day of the event to again confirm with her my arrival time. She sounded rushed on the big day. So I assured her that due to the Los Angeles traffic, it would take me the full twenty-five minutes to reach her apartment. Upon my arrival, I decided to call again instead of just knocking at her door. She answered the phone and seemed even more frazzled than before. I was hurried off the phone when she declared "I'll be right out!" Twenty-five minutes later while dozing in my car, the passenger side door swung open almost pulling it off the hinges. To my surprise a beautiful White woman not five-foot plopped in. She was extremely polite with curly reddish hair and clear water blue eyes. She quickly offered that she liked my car. "Me too" I said, figuring my cynicism was appropriate in mocking her disguised apology. She seemed familiar, but I figured it was because she could pass as a relative of actress Scarlett Johansson with her pale White skin. But this lady's voice yielded a foreign accent. How she knew which car to enter among the cluttered Hollywood sidewalk was a detail she somehow overcame. Our ride in the car was silent at first and the time was spent with me getting my bearings. I said nothing so she offered the same. I felt it was seasoned game considering modern day women usually reveal too much. She was definitely no amateur, and it was on me to begin the conversation.

We appeared as a car scene from *Driving Miss Daisy*. But I wore a Tweed Newsboy Beret, not a chauffeur's hat. Of course she sat up front beside me in my car. Also, this lady had a number tattooed on her forearm (51841) which seemed to contrast with her aristocratic appeal. Within moments conversation revealed that she had actually been a runaway who left her home in Vienna, Austria at nineteen. Her swift travels throughout Europe read like a cultured European playbill. Brief time with a friendly soldier had pushed her to New York City and eventually to Los Angeles. Anyway, I escorted her to the event and our relationship blossomed as they normally do with lunch, dinner, and movies. I always offered my arm and her dainty hands seemed to enjoy clutching it. We never mentioned people's stares when we ate at Will Smith's favorite Toluca Lake restaurant (Ca' De Sol) or arrived at films like *Atonement* which she predicted would win the Academy Award for Original Score. The fact that I was a mocha-man just shy of a foot-and-a- half taller and one-hundred-forty pounds heavier than her did not matter. This was a unique season of life, and we both decided to stop and smell the roses before it changed. She also had some food allergies like my wife. Oh, yeah, my wife. I should get to that.

My relationship with this lady had been going on a year when it became necessary that my wife meet her. I had been spending random off-hours with her and peak hours with my wife. This lady's name was Silvie. And my wife is an educated Black woman that does not play any mess. Since Silvie refused to drive, I picked her up the night of the meeting to bring her to my home for the introduction. I could not believe that there was no traffic on the freeway that night. Los Angeles traffic is usually 24/7. The drive took me forty-five minutes anyway. I needed the extra time to think through all of this.

The air seemed particularly brisk for a fall evening in Los Angeles. Despite that fact, I figured it not wise to just use my house key to enter our residence, with another woman in tow. Instead I knocked, offering my wife the respect due in these situations, and me the safety. There was no answer. Visions of my wife just beyond the wood framed door with Vaseline on her face and the Shun Gokuju Filet Knife we keep in the kitchen in hand became a serious thought. I looked at Silvie. As her uncertain eyes met mine it became evident that the forecast for the evening had changed a bit. I thought about manning up, but, instead swept the wetness from my face almost as quickly as it began to appear. To top it off I had seen the beautiful actress Lynn Whitfield on a plane a few days before. Scenes from her *A Thin Line Between Love and Hate* days began to attack my consciousness. I used a second knock on the door as a camouflage maneuver to step back from it just in case.

The seconds seemed like an eternity before the door abruptly opened, and the curious brown eyes of my wife looked Silvie down then up at me. I finally breathed and then smiled. Silvie was exactly what she had hoped for. And I figured her meeting Silvie would put to rest any concerns. My wife quickly lunged, pulling Silvie in from the burgeoning rain storm. The ladies began the sing-song chatter typical of old friends as they hugged and smiled graciously in a mutually respectful manner. See, Silvie knew all about my wife, and my wife had asked every single detail about Silvie. Their ability to interact so well on the first meeting seemed the result of two beautiful people rather than the Method of two great actresses. But who can tell the difference. The fact that Silvie was almost ninety years old, which was sixty years older than me and my wife did not seem to matter.

Silvie had lived many lives and seen many stolen too soon. She had endured camp Auschwitz and two others, knew three husbands, four languages, and many more fine wines and coffee houses on the Champs Elysees. She had even performed with Edith Piaf at the Moulin Rouge as part of The Golden Age of the theatre. Most of these things were written about in her autobiography, *Silvie*, which was endorsed on its cover by her friend Steven Spielberg. And although she never confirmed it, I believe to be the second Black man she had spent considerable time with since arriving in New York in the mid-1940's. At that time she had known famed actor Canada Lee. Why we were brought together at all for a season was unclear, but the time felt cozy, natural, and like the holidays.

As I painted Silvie's finger nails in the two star shared hospital room in Hollywood, she remained feisty, introspective, thoughtful, witty, and political. She was also unapologetic about calling Sarah Palin something similar to a "crazy witch" while glaring at her on the television. It had been twenty-five years since my bored sister convinced me to paint her nails. That occurred when I was young and innocent enough to figure that life lasted forever. Moments now had meaning. Immediately becoming a manicurist seemed the only way for me and Silvie to touch without acknowledging the gravity of the remaining time together. The political campaign on the television hanging from the ceiling did not obstruct the spectacular view of an enormous cross at the top of a church. It was the elephant in the room; although it was situated outside of the large cracked window directly within our fifth floor eye-line. Naturally I thought about some God talk, but found no words to say. Less would have to be more this time. Especially since there was less time for much more to be said. Besides, Silvie knew my thoughts on the matter. And the Jesus peace dangling from my neck always reiterated my position.

This entire story is all leading to one simple thing Silvie said within one of our trillions of conversations. I have no memory of our location or context of the statement. But, timing is key. Her statement was not profound or new to my ears, but it managed to unlock my thoughts and adjusted my perspective. "Make no mistake women have it much tougher than men in this world." It was a simple statement. Her look was stoic when she said it, although her eyes dared me to engage her in battle. My smile widened as I remained silent and considered her statement. It planted a seed within me to be more understanding of women's issues, to applaud those women that I love, and that have endured loving me. In that spirit my hope is to act as a special man for the marvelous women God has placed in my life. It will surely be shown in my variety of quirky ways. But hopefully it will leave an impact worth remembering and maybe even writing about. I believe that was at end the single greatest reason God placed Silvie in my life. Why I was in hers will remain unknown, although I had my beliefs in the matter.

A Warm December
Love Based Relationships

December comes for everybody. Although many human decisions preempt the temperature during that season, neither the ozone layer, nor the regions of residence have significance in the Decembers of life. They always come too often, especially the older you get. Even though it has mass advertisement as the most absolute part of the human experience, it remains shocking and only acceptable because it is impossible to change. Eternal transitions and sometimes those tremendous within life's navigation evoke the most genuine displays of love we know. Unfortunately, outpours are not regularly offered when time feels endless and the power of selflessness can be fully experienced. *A Warm December* is the greatest romantic love story ever told on film. Sure, I should mention *Ghost*, *The Notebook*, and heck I like *Two Can Play That Game*. The 1972 ambiance of A Warm December lacks the pageantry of modern cinema that captivates our senses through sensationalized sexuality, language, and drama. The film is of a Black romance set in England. The relationship is between a Black male doctor, recently widowed with a young daughter, and the mysterious niece of a prominent African Diplomat. What the story possesses is the selflessness that only true love embodies. *1 Corinthians 13* speaks about true love, not that cheap "I Love You" phrase heard from your last three boyfriends. Recognizing when it is, and understanding its power will allow you to not only experience the fullness that only love provides, but also dodge the phonies.

If I speak in the tongues[a] of men or of angels, but do not have love, I am only a resounding gong or a clanging cymbal. [2] If I have the gift of prophecy and can fathom all mysteries and all knowledge, and if I have a faith that can move mountains, but do not have love, I am nothing. [3] If I give all I possess to the poor and give over my body to hardship that I may boast,[b] but do not have love, I gain nothing.

[4] Love is patient, love is kind. It does not envy, it does not boast, it is not proud. [5] It does not dishonor others, it is not self-seeking, it is not easily angered, it keeps no record of wrongs. [6] Love does not delight in evil but rejoices with the truth. [7] It always protects, always trusts, always hopes, always perseveres.

[8] Love never fails. But where there are prophecies, they will cease; where there are tongues, they will be stilled; where there is knowledge, it will pass away. [9] For we know in part and we prophesy in part, [10] but when completeness comes, what is in part disappears. [11] When I was a child, I talked like a child, I thought like a child, I reasoned like a child. When I became a man, I put the ways of childhood behind me. [12] For now we see only a reflection as in a mirror; then we shall see face to face. Now I know in part; then I shall know fully, even as I am fully known.

[13] And now these three remain: faith, hope and love. But the greatest of these is love.

(1 Corinthians 13 NIV)

Love is the most powerful tool in which we can access. Discovering what love is can provide a pragmatic approach to being love and embracing its fullness. That notion however in romance is reserved for only the mature and discerning. The reason is because physical, material, and status attractions bring about yearnings so tremendous that most people fall for the okey doke. Anyone interested in fulfillment within a sustainable relationship however must seek self development which leads to maturity and discernment. Sure, the Obama Special (three chicken wings and a waffle) at *Roscoe's Chicken and Waffles,* with a side of macaroni and cheese is delicious. It looks, smells, and taste much better than carrots, celery, and a side of ranch. But, to eat the Obama Special regularly without acknowledging its adverse affect on your health is not a smart decision. Basically, you will eventually look, feel, and therefore act greasy. Trust that everything that looks good is not good for you. Do not pay a high price for a cheap thrill.

Mo' Money
The Relationships Between Black Men, Black Women, and Money

Not being able to financially provide is a challenge for many Black men. Many Black men are able to muster three hots and a cot for their woman. The challenge is that Black people now get married later in life. Educated Black women's median marriage age is thirty-something. By that time these women rather those hots to be after valet parking and the cot upon a mahogany sleigh bed-frame. Educated Black women are often accustomed to high-end lifestyles that they plan to build upon. To begin compromising that lifestyle and provide headship to a man with lesser means becomes tricky (especially dependent upon how much lesser). I get it. But educated Black women must be careful to not let finances become the central factor when gauging a potential mate. Allow his ambition, faith, and values to lead the analysis. Money and titles can be fleeting, but connecting with a man that has integrity provides something money cannot buy. Remember, that is exactly why you still desire a man. Some educated Black women may say "I will not be happy downsizing my lifestyle." Or, "I cannot respect a man who does not make more money." The assessment is all about "I". If that is the case then self development and biblical perspective is needed before being ready to engage an authentic relationship that can stand the test of time. Those ideologies put money as heaven and life about making it rain. Although that attitude may keep an educated Black woman financially well above water, it heightens the probability of her soaring as a Black Swan (Strong Woman Achiever, No Spouse). You should gradually get an understanding of his earning potential, debts, resume, credit score, salary, savings, 401k, and all else that will affect your quality of life. Those things matter. Just keep in mind that as you add up his dough or subtract from your own, that money cannot buy you love (But, I did recently here of a Brother that said "They say money can't buy love. But you find me a woman with money and I'll love her to death"). One advantage of marrying well fairly young and building careers and finances together is that both people prayerfully, financially, and emotionally are invested in the climb to the top. It is naturally different when a companion shows up at the eleventh hour.

Many geeky boys grow up to be educated Black men with solid potential to be committed husbands. Although these men may not have the alluring bravado of around-the-way men, they are in it top level careers and getting paid well. But even many of the graduate school geeks struggle to attain an idea of success that gives them confidence to settle down. Mass media fantasies at every glance heighten the definition of what a provider and manhood should be. This has a particularly negative effect on Black male securities since most are products of a single female upbringing and lean toward what society says for male influence and confidence. The result is that they correctly correlate husbandry with providing, but have completely fixated on money, leaving the value of providing in spirit, time, and support absent. Do not get me wrong, the television culture has been a gift to Black agendas at times. Noteworthy illustrations were during civil rights eras as documented in books such as *And the Walls Come Tumbling Down*, or documentaries like *Keep Your Eyes on the Prize.* Otherwise, it has largely meandered from *Amos and Andy* to the fantasies of girth and riches of sports figures, and fictional rap videos. Now I like watching old Amos and Andy shows and some rap videos. But with television representations being so impactful on the mindsets of people watching, balanced representations are particularly necessary for minorities.

An added angst affecting Black male sensibilities is that educated Black women that educated Black men want to impress can often ascend within the corporate structure more quickly. Also educated Black men's counterparts (White men) usually have similar credentials, but often provide amazing luxuries for their families due to financial and political inheritances. White professional men always speak about being on the lake, at the country-club, in the mountains, traveling abroad, or aboard The Disney Fantasy cruise ship. To cry a river for Brothers will not help. Educated Black men do not like sympathy. It can be felt as emasculating from women that they want to lead. Strong men prefer to feel like warriors not victims. Educated Black men can appreciate acknowledgement of some unfortunate truths regarding their plight in living the American Dream. They also want to feel that the woman that they care about is in their corner. That does not mean that a woman should always agree with what the man is saying. That is not being progressive. But remember that an educated Black man wants to be even more successful than you want him to be. He may just be trying to find his way. The tone and timing of how an educated Black woman communicates with an educated Black man will make the difference in how the information is received. Effective communication is essential for any relationship to flourish.

When relationships are bounded by *Negro Spirituals* instead of materials, financial agendas can be placed in proper perspective. There is much more to a healthy relationship than money. Progress requires a collective attempt by educated Black women and educated Black men to do better. Being sensitive to the unique circumstances of each other can produce the foundation for power couples to build families.

The bottom line is that most Black men want to be *The New H.N.I.C.* which is admirable. They want to be the bread winner within their relationship and most women prefer that as the ideal too. It is human nature for a man to want to provide for his woman, and for a woman to want her man to provide. Sure, many women want to make their own cheese (money). But it is obviously quite nice if the man getting the milk is making the cake. Black men not being able to provide some of the finer things in life is not a new phenomenon in Black families. But generations X and Y have been tremendously impacted by social media, mass media, and examples of incredibly wealthy Blacks. And whether ridin'dirty or riding clean some of these people are really shining. We used to rap with Andre and Big Boi on *Elevators* about Cadillac doz (Cadillac, $35,000 - $90,000). Now we listen to Maybach Music (Maybach, $350,000 – 1,000,000). The glamorous life is undoubtedly magnified in our society more than ever. From *MTV Cribs* to *How'd you get so Rich*, it is easy to watch *The Fabulous Life of...*and develop "champagne wishes and caviar dreams." Not rectified for the majority of Black people is the financial, educational, systematic, and familial enhancements needed to align with these increased expectations. In many of these categories the situation has actually worsened. This can leave Blacks very susceptible to being left broke, busted, and disgusted! Progress is best approached from the heartfelt understanding that current circumstances may not necessarily be part of the dream for the educated Black man or woman. Therefore navigation of Black relationships within current society must usually still have some vision of "we shall over-come" instead of the feeling that "we have arrived." Overcoming obstacles together can really bond a relationship.

Men often feel that if they only had more money their problems would be solved. Maybe it would provide some relief. But remember the song *Mo Money Mo Problems* was one of The Notorious B.I.G.'s posthumous hits. Money can quickly attract greater pressures, gold-diggers, and hardships. Unfortunately in many cases money is valued beyond character-values that could lead to a relationship of value. It is hard for people to understand *the best things in life are free* type slogans, *Philippians 4:11* or even *4:6*. Cash is supposedly needed now to vacillate among those that can avoid public schools, housing, transportation, assistance, and intoxication. I get it. But beware, because even if money is acquired, financial and biblical values become the crucial steps in not tripping up your relationship.

Friends, Lovers, and Soul Mates
The Complexities of Relationships

Educated Black women endure characterizations that often create a difficult positioning for romance. Their options for companionship usually narrow as they ascend economically and professionally. This is due to their financial and professional progress being coupled with existing stereotypes that all contest the male ego. It is true that Black women have traditionally been forced to push, pull, and fight to exist at a humane level. A strong and enduring spirit has therefore been embedded within educated Black women. Unfortunately, men have created unfair standards for women that infiltrate the minds of our society. Although changing, it is of the weaker, submissive female vessel in need of male protection, guidance, and strength. *Missing White Woman Syndrome* has always showcased advanced value to White women's existence within larger society. This has often left educated Black women to be characterized as brash, intimidating, and having masculine assertiveness. Both stereotypes are unfair, although not without some legitimate examples. That is the case with most stereotypes. In a male dominated society, ideals are perpetuated that allow men to feel bigger, stronger, smarter, and more heroic than actually true.

Many Black women have experienced many situations that cause dissatisfaction with men in general. Some others unfortunately allow negative experiences expressed by friends to get within their psyche. Both options lead to a hardened heart that unfairly indicts new possibly positive men that enter the scene. Before long, Angry Black Woman Syndrome becomes less a stupid insult and moreso actual symptoms being projected. At root these women feel emotions like hurt, sadness, loneliness, unattractiveness, fear, instability, or bitterness. Symptoms then manifest into blame and anger towards men that they want to attract. Protection against being hurt and being played is natural. But, hurt people, hurt people. Wounds must heal so that they do not booby trap new relationships. If in a relationship, negative feelings can easily transition into insecurities and eventually petty disputes and strife. Without sincere acknowledgement of the root cause, moving toward happiness is impossible.

It is often thought that men actively seek the attention of random women; however fulfillment is needed by all individuals regardless of gender. Even a good man can gradually become unfulfilled, underappreciated, and in need. Any person can become a sitting duck for misconduct when there is a void in their relationship, especially with dogs, cats, cubs, gerbils, cougars, wolves, horses, and cocks on the hunt for easy prey. Analyze a man for who he is. It should be someone that you respect and trust if entering a relationship. Although it is better to give than receive, do not give everything at once. Allow it to be a mutually reciprocal relationship. It can then take root with a stronger possibility of blossoming into something special.

Many women live in fear that their man is going to cheat. But fear tolerated is faith contaminated. Plus, why would God send you a cheating husband? That's the reason to pray for God to match you with a mate instead of finding one for yourself. Yes, we are all aware of relationships were there has been adultery. Reality is that sins sometimes happen since we are all born sinners. Although there are no guarantees, never should negativity be expected from a Godsend. The devil is a lie! If a woman in a relationship has that constant fear then that man is the wrong choice, she knows of differences in expectations, or has unresolved issues that are being brought into the relationship.

Let me be clear on this next point. Men do love sex. Some men enjoy it more than others and have multiple ideas on what is satisfactory. These things should be discussed and women should be sincere within this communication. If not, it is sure to be an ongoing problem that will be difficult to cope with. Men are easily pestered with wandering thoughts when it is cold inside and women are dropping it like it is hot outside. Compatibility helps keep the covers un-tucked and the curtains closed.

Men can eventually tell if a woman is not a sincere participant in sexual relations. Fulfillment for both persons is essential in this category. It is very significant to his nature, manhood, and ultimately the relationship. It is very significant to a woman's nature, womanhood, and ultimately the relationship. If either is consistently unfulfilled it will hamper the emotional connection. The lack of an emotional connection will hamper fulfillment in the bedroom. Things then turn scandalous and alternative thoughts easily turn into fantasies, dreams, and dirty little secrets. Be honest with him and yourself in this category. Do not agree to do extra credit if it is laborious for you to finish basic assignments. You will be doomed to fail and he will be enticed to rise. There is a brick house on every block, and that little pig will be happy to let him sneak in the backdoor. Have lengthy conversations during the courting process. This will help you to determine if you want to play dress up and be the headliner in the opening credits. If not, fine. You should not live your life uncomfortably. But know that if you are not honest about these things, then it will become natural for you to feel that he may go knocking.

Do not ever underestimate a man's attractiveness to beautiful women. And since studies suggest that women in general are getting more beautiful it is no surprise men take notice. Healthy relationships are not based on physicality alone. Those in that situation should beware. Personalities, insecurities, expectations, physicality, education, timing, and other considerations all play a part in merging expected and unexpected combinations. The man you like is most likely monogamous out of choice, not lack of options. Do not be like Jackie on *Basketball Wives*, paranoid of your man's every move. No self respecting man wants to be mothered by his woman. Black men particularly hate being accused of things when there is no tradition of due process. Accusations need to be founded because it will affect trust within the relationship. A man who constantly feels he must always pay the piper will eventually feel that he might as well get it unclogged. Do not be surprised that if you treat him like a convict, it may awaken some convictions. Men want to be respected and valued. If those things are stripped he is not empowered to face the world with a sense of responsibility to the relationship. I am not saying be stupid. Some dudes are just players. Nor am I suggesting that you act *Legally Blonde*, like Scarlett O'Hara, or Christmas Snow. But, when individuals are exhausted within a relationship they are left vulnerable. If you truthfully do not trust a particular man then you are playing yourself by being with him. Or, if you are carrying baggage of hurt, get therapy so you can be well and learn to trust again.

Strange Fruit
Homosexuality's Relationship with Black America

It was the late 1990's when my second-cousin got married. To my surprise, my brother Ice and I were asked to be groomsmen. We were both honored to have received the invitation. On the Friday before the ceremony we gassed up the Honda Prelude, and left Chattanooga headed down I-40. To accommodate our long legs we reclined the car seats as if at the spa. We needed to be comfortable. Then Ice cranked the air conditioner to remain on chill despite the April sunrays. Set for the leisurely drive, we raced down the highway. As usual on south bound road trips, we stopped to stock up on snacks. Ice snatched a Watchamacalit and had a Big Gulp full of soda before I had even found the Reese's Peanut Butter Cups. The repositioning of the Jungle Juices slowed this Quick Trip. And the middle-eastern store clerk at the front seemed to be irritated that we were even in the store. After scanning the entire catalog of refrigerated drinks the lion emblem on the red Jungle Juice carton appeared. The Jungle Juices had been right in front of me the whole time. I could not figure out why the clerk did not say that when I yelled to ask him where they were. What a schmuck! I paused, contradicting my routine of just grabbing one. I had now been exposed to some other possibilities. I decided on an alternative fruit drink instead.

I popped the top and took a big swallow of the strange fruit drink while approaching the front counter. The drink was trapped in my cheeks when I raised the bottle and eyeballed it with the sourpuss face reserved for brown Listerine. It was nasty compared to my usual choice. So I made a quick right turn and spat without gargling out front of the store. I had good reason not to pay for the drink. And had it been a few years prior, the store clerk would have been told with profanity that he should not have had that nasty shit in stock. But we were college men now, and bits of maturity had slid in. I dropped some coins on the counter to pay the clerk. But he did not like how I did it. I could feel him staring at me as I was strutting out the door. He actually mumbled something at me too. I looked back at him. He looked at me stone faced. The film *Menace II Society* provided a similar opening scene earlier that decade. But this was real-life. A bad decision could mean dire consequences. I needed to make the right decision.

Despite the drink drama, Ice and I were deep into conversations of the usual politics while in the car that continued into the store. It was lightweight stuff—hoes, sports, hip-hop, women, God, money, Black People, niggaz, and The White Man. Things were usually addressed in that order. These conversations were not done in a manner particularly coherent by other patrons, but through a vernacular, drawls, and southern slang specific to us—me at least. We would somewhat rearrange the content of our conversations years later.

The scene with me and the middle-eastern clerk ended without incident. Ice had hustled back to the car after leaving the store. His looking at me with an ambiguous smile did not stop me from laughing at the shiny perspiration he wiped from his forehead. It was like he was thawing out. Ice told me not to sweat the clerk next time. I said "who's sweating?" Ice drove first since it was his car. I relaxed and karaoked the poetry of my inner city brethren. The CD disc changer had been loaded with albums I felt were Five Mics (The term is from Source magazine's rating scale of hip-hop albums). *The Lost Tapes* was of course the founding father of the group. But I also spoke astrology with *Aquemini*, global warming with *Hell on Earth*, Black Power with Black Star and *Life After Death* with Biggie. When I drove, Ice would read a book called *Who Stole my Cheese*. But not without rocking his head to the beats like in a Methodist church. My head knock was more COGIC. This scene played out for hours. To change it up I would EQ the sounds a bit to slide in jokes about him reading on the trip. But he brushed my comments off as usual. Ice had been changing over the previous months and even made remarks about making a law school bid. He had a cold way of running something by me without asking directly my thoughts. But he always wanted to know my opinion. I offered that the law thing sounded cool to me and that it was encouraging to hear him slide toward a career where he may one day just chill.

A few years later Ice was President of the Black Law School Association in law school. He was also responsible for bringing Johnny Cochran to town as key note commencement speaker. Many White people were still pissed-off about the O.J. Simpson trial at that time. Bringing the attorney that successfully defended O.J. stirred up a few people at the southern school. Anyway, I imagined Ice and Johnny Cochran chilling in the back seat of the limo. Ice arranged it to show him the city of Knoxville. I picture that they were popping bottles of

Cristal, toasting to Johnny's past, and planning Ice's future. For the few hours before the commencement ceremony, Johnny served as the ideal protégé so Ice could become a cold lawyer.

Back to the wedding story, Clear Water, Florida was the wedding destination. After the lengthy trip we grabbed our tuxedo bags and strolled from the parking lot into a hotel that provided the wedding party's group rate. The rehearsal dinner was that night which justified my earlier speeding ticket. We needed to move expeditiously since my great aunts would be cooking the meal. Those Alabama gals could throw down when it came to cooking like on *Soul Food*. It was just beyond dawn upon our arrival and there appeared to be a fraternity convention at the hotel. Black men were everywhere. The only uncertainty stemmed from the fact that they wore no unified colors or paraphernalia. "Strange," I thought. We were frat dudes too and had been to conventions, regional meetings, and all else that put us at least at a masters level of that scene. It was nice to have finally arrived however, and the bevy of Brothers out and about helped put us at ease.

Just a few years prior we made a similar trip to Cocoa Beach, Florida to deliver our sister to a NASA internship. That experience offered several racially motivated interactions that were very off- putting within the 24-hours we were in that city. Coincidentally or not it had left a state impression (R.I.P. Trayvon Martin). We immediately knew this trip would be different.

Okay, back to the parking-lot of the wedding story. The whistling was not obnoxious but obviously to get our attention. We stopped and focused on where the whistling came from. There were three dudes chilling at an old-school Cutlass Supreme. All were big and kind of scruffy with a street chic look. But they put you more in the mindset of Tyler Perry than Idris Alba. Two of them were posted up out front of the car while the one smiling was chilling in the passenger's seat with the door open. We looked at them, they looked at us –nothing. The chuckle from the guy in the passenger's seat retying his bandana was the only movement. Did these cats want Beef? It was an unusual vibe but we obeyed street etiquette and stared just long enough to put to rest any question of intimidation, but not in a manner to insinuate confrontation. We were outnumbered and far from our turf. I turned to continue toward the hotel when the bewildered look that reappeared during my viewing of the film *Brokeback Mountain*, first appeared on my face. I stopped abruptly and looked back at my brother who had gotten hip to the game more quickly. His face looked perplexed but more like he had been cussed out; and this time his sweat signified that he may come completely unthawed. He cut his eyes toward me and we had a meeting of the minds that was quite different than the preference of these dudes. I was glad my brother looked like the handsome actor Leon and hoped that I resembled the unsightly musician Shabba Ranks.

We moved on to the hotel but assessed the scene through very different lens. Brothers everywhere were flirting and scoping. Entering the lobby a pitch Black guy five-foot-three, wearing only cut-off Daisy Duke's sashayed past us. It was his scene, not ours, and he eagerly maximized his visibility in the marketplace. My feelings were multifaceted during the experience. I felt objectified, irritated, and misunderstood when moving about among the group. Quite similar to how Kim Kardashian looked as if she felt at the 2012 BET Awards. Not comfortable enough with the assumed judgment to want to appear "at home" but uncomfortable enough to act un-phased. Reality was that few people probably even cared about our presence. But in those moments that felt like a few too many. It is nice to have lived, learned, and matured since that time.

If you are from So Ho, We Ho, No Ho, Boystown, South End, The Short North, GaYbor, Asbury Park, Pier Head, and a host of other gayborhoods with names not so overblown, you are familiar with a lifestyle traditionally not embraced in larger America. Now networks like Bravo and Logo offer flaming personalities like Derek J, Miss Lawrence, and RuPaul. Even openly gay syndicated talk show hosts like Ellen, Nate, Robin Roberts, Anderson Cooper, and Don Lemon provide news, comedy, interior design, politics and other tremendous commentary. It should not be necessary for me to give props to individuals with obvious talents. However, Americans ostracizing homosexuals from basic civil rights have a long and strong history. Evolving politics now lends itself to a more equitable conversation on the national platform.

Black America has been even slower to gain perspective on homosexuality. I would encourage Christians to listen to the song *Same Love* and consult the Holy Bible for themselves before voting on this issue. For Black women it may seem like another phenomenon stealing potential romantic partners. That feeling is natural. But the ability for men to be forthright with their sexuality helps gay and switch-hitters to not feel pressured to enter heterosexual relationships. These developments in our society help Black women to move toward honest, happy, and healthy relationships. Count it all joy, but keep your gaydar handy as down-low Brothers remain actively underground. Because although Terri McMillan got her groove back, remember that her hubby was getting his groove on –with Tyrone.

Roots
The Relationship Between Self and Circumstances

Roots the television miniseries is one of the most important works within the visual arts. It provides the needed glimpse of the path to "freedom" that had been lost in the complex plight of African Americans. Unfortunately it is not usually shown to kids and is not mentioned in our schools. Even the book version of Roots is not usually a summer reading assignment. Just as *The Diary of Anne Frank* finds its way into American curriculums to teach about Jewish persecution, significant African American stories that chart our path should be included. It is often said that a picture is worth one-thousand words. So imagine what all can be taken away from the 9.5 hours that makes up the Roots television miniseries (Paperback book 912 pages). The television series was watched by over 130 million Americans. The book version of Roots was #1 on the New York Times Best Seller list for 22 weeks. Author Alex Haley did an amazing job bringing us what is considered one of the most important works of the 20th Century. But the incredible reception of the book in 1976 and television miniseries in 1977 neither translated into sustaining programs nor reparations for the killing, rape, free labor, and psychological damage thrust onto African Americans. I will leave that alone to focus on what we can do for ourselves now.

Black culture has evolved within Western society. But broken families, bondage, supposed freedom, fear, and all else inhumane were uniquely thrust upon Black ancestors and trickles down to Black romantic relationships today. The film series showed some good White folks, happiness, triumph, and family among the slaves too. But am I to applaud the establishment for basic humanity? Okay, really, I am stepping off the soap box.

Here is where I am going with this: Historical and current family dynamics are very significant to what you attract as a companion. It is very difficult for most people to identify personal shortcomings. This is because they have inevitably been produced from the influences held most dear. Despite all your good traits, bad traits also originate from family, friends, and your neighborhood. All these traits contribute to your attractiveness and abilities within a relationship. Admit it, negative traits of loved ones sneak in as part of your DNA. The bottom line is that the apple does not fall far from the tree. If your family tree is barren of fruitful relationships, or exudes drama, then it is probable that you are an at-risk companion. That's okay. Acknowledgement is the first step to making different choices. Just know that self development is required before being ready to identify a positive relationship or hold on to one.

It is humbling to make a true self assessment in understanding what is not working in career and general social circumstances. This is even more difficult when assessing characteristics that are detrimental to attracting and sustaining a romantic relationship that makes you happy. Why? It is extremely personal! It is much easier to shift blame to a multitude of other factors beyond self.

Educated Black women who are serious about attracting and sustaining a long term relationship must be willing to do a self assessment. You can then get to the root of what may be blocking your blessing. From that point you can begin to make different decisions which will create a different result.

Many Black women do not know five couples that exemplify the type of companionship and family that they would like to model. But we all remember The Cosby Show which sure gave us an ideal. Increasingly, Black women (and men) are products of single parent homes, divorced homes, parent separation, and other scenarios that did not exemplify the type of committed relationship you want to establish. Maybe you were raised with a single mother or father that had various companions during your childhood. Or maybe you grew up with a relative. It could be that your father was absent and you grew up without brothers. Therefore you have limited reference for the basic gender differences obvious when in close proximity to men for a time. You may have even been the product of infidelity, abuse, abandonment, or other unfortunate circumstances. Let us not even entertain your personal relationship experiences that probably add to your multitude of challenges. I know what you are thinking. That's life! True. And it should not be expected to be perfect. It is also life that most relationships break up or hang on without a true connection. The goal is for your relationship to be exceptional. So in short, check yourself before you wreck yourself. That is the first step in doing your part.

Black Saga (For Men)
Black Men Navigating New Familial Responsibilities

Manhood today is difficult for even well intentioned Black men. There are many new-age challenges to deal with. For some Brothers the sky looks so unlimited that they underestimate the necessity for hard work, and reach nowhere. Many other Brothers struggle for access to resources and how to overcome the norms of what usually happens to men from their neighborhood. These are just two possibilities. Challenges are often in more sophisticated and systematic forms today. These challenges are also thrust among human rights, children's rights, civil rights, gay rights, women's rights, Latino rights, religious rights, animal rights, and all other left wing politics trying to fly. It is true that Black people find justice within many of these categories. But these politics also dilute the unfulfilled proclamations for Black masses. The result is needy Black families, children, schools, and neighborhoods that all wither away without adequate direct attention. More educated Black men are needed to help lead the charge in making progress.

The stakes continue to rise as tuition, the cost of housing and food, divorce, suicide, drop-out rates, babies out of wedlock, and unemployment do too. Greater preparation is needed to understand how to get a piece of the American Dream. But morale is slipping away. Family dynamics are now so crumbled that individuals that choose marriage and its responsibilities must possess great maturity. Many men are choosing their personal motives and selfish ambitions over family.

Relationships are one of the few challenges of life in which people accept advice willy-nilly. It is a common mistake. Those with little success in their own love lives are able to establish themselves within the public consciousness as experts on the matter. People need to beware of such. I mean, I love watching Patti Stranger's show on Bravo. But the fact that she is the *Millionaire Matchmaker* without personally being matched with a millionaire should not make cents.

Juice

The families Black men marry into will likely be similar to their own –full of women. Many of these women have endured complex histories with men who have fallen short of their responsibilities. Or it may be full of women that blame men for their dissatisfaction. It is not unusual for a Black male to find himself the lone man in his new extended family. Other Black male figures may be present, but lack the leadership qualities necessary to push forward. And although the many single women within this acquired family are long standing contributors to the development of this fine woman, it is necessary that each man serves as ultimate visionary for his own family. That should be the deal when wifey takes on the new surname. If not, good luck. If your wife refuses to take on your surname at all, then you all may have some bigger issues, so good riddance. There are occasions when a woman has built her name within professional circles where it becomes advantageous to the family for her to keep her maiden name and just add yours. It also seems reasonable if a woman chooses to relinquish her middle name and bump her maiden name into that slot. It is not about cutting her identify from loved ones. It is fair that she has feelings and relationships that she may want to preserve. So Brothers need to get up from the ego trip. It is necessary that two become one and the name change is symbolic of her commitment to your headship and the unified family identity being significant and respected within social, business, and political arenas. Some women will contest that this is antiquated thinking. If she says that, then remind her that the engagement ring with the exact carat, clarity, color, and cut she wants you to buy is too, along with the idea that you should even wear a wedding ring. She may begin to see things a bit differently.

Women are quick to start running things within relationships. This is why educated Black men must put their house in order. Biblically based traditions of commitment, roles, and vows should be upheld. Remind her that if she has a problem with it then she should try *Conversations with God* and allow him to provide perspective. Because, rest assured that when stuff hits the fan, she will look at you as not having provided proper leadership; and, it will likely be true. Be a man by first planting biblically based seeds that will allow your relationship and family to flourish. The divine foundation is the only way to flush out many of the kinks that linger or cause the demise of many relationships.

Men, it is your job to let your actions showcase your leadership abilities as visionary, provider, and God fearing man. The most acclaimed Black visionaries have been empowered by God. X, Robeson, and King all are the sons of preachers. President Obama explained that by working with Black churches as a community organizer, he grew to understand the power of the African American religious tradition. He is now a devout Christian. There is power in the blood of Jesus.

The Help

Many educated Black women of today have no desire to address domestic duties nor have they acquired any experience in doing them. Although most men consistently want at least a good meat loaf and some clean drawers, it becomes the norm to go out and eat or to afford cleaning crews. Beware of continuously paying for duties that usually help crazy glue the bond that will be needed to sustain the relationship. When couples do things for each other it begins to strengthen that fabric of a home and a family. I am not saying not to enjoy some luxuries. But you may one day feel that if the nanny is doing the cooking, cleaning, and raising the kids that you may have been wise to have married her. That is exactly what comedian Robin Williams did. Do not underestimate the need for doing the work necessary to strengthen a marriage; literally. Having said that, encourage your wife in a manner that she wants to meet the standard. Set the standard by being responsible for the cars, cutting the yard, answering the front door, sitting at the head of the table, praying out loud over dinner, having your voice on the home answering machine, making the dinner reservations under your name, exercising, arranging quality time, driving the family to church, and other duties that can help set a standard worthy of your wife's respect. Basically, stop talking and start doing. Leaders lead. So lead in giving and you will be positioned for her to want to give it to you –and both of you will be happy. If not, your prodding will fall on deaf ears.

Men, find good marriage peer groups and couples ministries at church. These groups will increase your bond and provide perspective and increased appreciation of your contribution and vice versa. Your bond will also grow stronger spiritually. This will empower you to sincerely appreciate her feelings; but not endure her in a manner where you are expected to take a lot of mess, and spend your time answering loaded questions. Remember, "What the Higher Man seeks is in himself, what the lower man seeks is in others" (Confucius | Our Oriental Heritage, 1935).

What's Love Got to Do With It
Unfortunate Truths About Relationships

"Many a man owes his success to his first wife and his second wife to his success" (Jim Backus). Young, gifted, shallow men marry a smart gal, get older, acquire money, and then trade in their starter wife for a new model. Young, beautiful, materialistic women marry for the money, grow older, lose the man, keep half the money, but struggle finding further companionship (depending on how much money kept). Sure, these are unfair but familiar generalizations. They could be interpreted as women getting the brunt of these events; or, that women really have first dibs to push aside the profusion of mediocre and horny dudes for a man of substance. Carelessness with such a time sensitive opportunity to be the chooser is easily squandered as time gradually allows the tables to turn. Or immaturity in the selection process causes later trepidation. Some ministers argue that it is largely because women are not the natural chooser and quote Proverbs 18:22 *He who finds a wife finds a good thing and obtains favor from the Lord.* It may be something to literally consider. But that biblical advice was provided by King Solomon who had a few hundred wives and a few hundred more mistresses. Go figure. Either way, as educated Black women look back on college's access to educated Black men, it is amazing how the greatest opportunity to identify a husband type was presented at a time when mature vision may not have been available. Instead, youth and incorrect standards may have led to ostentatious dudes rather than a husband type man.

The relationship game never changes which means to some degree it can be learned. You can gain understanding by dissecting relationships. But be careful. Dissecting them in excess can become frustrating and counterproductive. Pursing relationships from a godly perspective provides wisdom, and without godly reasoning, saltiness can overly season possibilities of a great relationship.

The allure of beauty for men and power for women has been documented since biblical days. Although it may seem shallow, it is reality. It is the game most people indulge in on some level. If the current cinematic trends are not in line with a particular woman's beauty, she should not fret. Observations of attractiveness are not only generalizations but some definitions vary over time and by culture. For instance, throughout Africa many years ago, really large women and those with enormous ears were considered loveliest. In other African cultures men would line their women up and pick from those that extend the furthest backside. See, some things change and others not so much. It is hard for some women to accept that physical beauty not always the greatest factor in attracting their dream man. But everyone reading this sentence knows women that are gorgeous, single, hardened, lonely, and confused. These women have fallen victim to men with games and gimmicks beyond their experience. They may have options, but are now susceptible to entertaining men that offer headaches or heartache.

I do understand the strength of inherent desires when choosing a mate. Do not get the lustful feelings that spur on thoughts of a one night roll in the hay confused with long term companionship characteristics. Your base desires should be met on some level. But not weighed to where the metrics of future happiness is off tilt. Those that choose superficially easily become enthralled with their vice desire. That makes it extremely challenging for them to step away from a bad relationship. For instance, for a gold digging woman to give up a man providing a high standard of living is extremely difficult despite the fact he may have five other girlfriends. She will bitch and moan. But at the end of the day she often stays, looking pitiful. Mimi on Love & Hip-Hop was an example of how being attached to an individual without similar core values can gradually evolve into an unfortunate existence. Since she did not initially accept that her man was a player, she was ultimately trapped in a toxic and embarrassing relationship.

The key to recognizing a relationship worth sustaining is by examining the character traits of your potential mate. That takes patience, supplication, and being able to accept the reality of who that person is. Don't let superficial or material things impact the clarity of vision needed for a mature, happy relationship.

It is common to see a woman enter a toxic relationship out of desperation, and actually believe that it will have a fairytale ending. For instance, a woman that has accepted the role of a mistress is silly to think the man will leave his main squeeze, hook up with her, and be a monogamous

partner. The chances of that are simply not in her favor.
That is why it is best not to play with fire. A smooth man
may whisper sweet nothings. But words have always been
as cheap and easy as the women actually listening to them.
It is not the attention from a man that should be significant,
but under what premise and context in which the
relationship takes shape. Easy come easy go.

The Mis-Education of the Negro
Relationships Between Educated Black People & Black Thought

Throughout our lifetime Bill Cosby has been relevant. His
projects have always provided interesting perspective. *Fat
Albert, Little Bill, Uptown Saturday Night, Bill Cosby:
Himself,* and of course *The Cosby Show* where his
picturesque wife had the exact amount of sugar and spice
are only among his many productions. I applaud even his
social and political attempts through books, music, and
speeches although I do not always agree with him. I do not
always agree with my mother, or anyone else for that
matter. For instance the origin of his rap CD, *Bill Cosby
Presents The Cosnarati: State Of Emergency*, seemed
genuine, but to me it was absolutely terrible. But his book
Come on People should be a text assigned by Black parents
to their teenagers, to exhale just a bit after reading Paul
Robeson's *Here I Stand.* Unfortunately, an implication that
most Black people will hear his rap album instead of a read
of his book is not just a stereotype.

In July of 1968, CBS began airing a documentary series
with the first segment called *Black History: Lost, Stolen, or
Strayed.* Cosby, the young host of the show was hip,
current, and eradicated stereotypes for the 60 minute
program. He used the time to pull Black history and

education from the abyss, and dissed actor Stepin Fetchit for stepping and fetching. In the documentary, Cosby was clearly more Clarence 13X (founder of the Five-Percent movement) than Clarence Thomas. And as the book *Our Kind of People* noted, he would not fit in with the Black bourgeoisie of Philadelphia. He looked more like he preferred the *US Organization* of Los Angeles.

By the 1990's, Cosby's image was defined largely by the "respectable" Heathcliff Huxtable character he portrayed on The Cosby Show. His hairline was evaporating which added to his evolution into an on-screen character applauded by larger audiences. In real life he had completed his doctorate of education degree. That was a commendable accomplishment considering the demands of his remarkable entertainment career. Equipped with his doctorate and his years of fortune and fame, Cosby now serves as a unique voice with mixed interpretations from Black audiences. The founder of the North Carolina School of the Arts provided relevant insight pertaining to the need to collaborate both personal and artistic advancements. "It is not enough to be trained as an artist, but as a person. As an artist you will express yourself as a person and the richer you are as a person the better your expression will be" (Vittorio Giannini). At the two hundred dollar per plate, May 2004 NAACP awards ceremony in Washington, D.C., the affluent Cosby used many expressions to commemorate the 50th anniversary of the Brown v. Board of Education Supreme Court decision. Here is the gist of it:

Ladies and gentlemen…I heard a prize fight manager say to his fellow who was losing badly, "David, listen to me.

It's not what's he's doing to you. It's what you're not doing." (laughter)

Ladies and gentlemen, these people sat, they opened the doors, they gave us the right, and today, ladies and gentlemen, in our cities and public schools we have fifty percent drop out. In our own neighborhood, we have men in prison. No longer is a person embarrassed because they're pregnant without a husband. (clapping) No longer is a boy considered an embarrassment if he tries to run away from being the father of the unmarried child. (clapping)

Ladies and gentlemen, the lower economic and lower middle economic people are not holding their end in this deal. In the neighborhood that most of us grew up in, parenting is not going on. (clapping)...

I'm talking about these people who cry when their son is standing there in an orange suit. Where were you when he was two? (clapping)...Where were you when he was eighteen, and how come you don't know he had a pistol? (clapping) And where is his father...And why doesn't the father show up to talk to this boy?

The church is only open on Sunday. And you can't keep asking Jesus to do things for you (clapping). You can't keep asking that God will find a way. God is tired of you (clapping and laughing). God was there when they won all those cases. 50 in a row. That's where God was because these people were doing something...

We cannot blame white people (clapping)...white people don't live over there. They close up the shop early. The

Korean ones still don't know us as well...they stay open 24 hours. (laughter)...

These people want to buy the friendship of a child....and the child couldn't care less. Those of us sitting out here who have gone on to some college or whatever we've done, we still fear our parents. (clapping and laughter) And these people are not parenting. They're buying things for the kid. $500 sneakers, for what? They won't buy or spend $250 on Hooked on Phonics. (clapping)

...People getting shot in the back of the head over a piece of pound cake! Then we all run out and are outraged, "The cops shouldn't have shot him" What the hell was he doing with the pound cake in his hand? (laughter and clapping) I wanted a piece of pound cake just as bad as anybody else (laughter) And I looked at it and I had no money. And something called parenting said if get caught with it you're going to embarrass your mother...You're going to embarrass your family.

Brown Versus the Board of Education is no longer the white person's problem. We've got to take the neighborhood back (clapping) ...Just forget telling your child to go to the Peace Corps. It's right around the corner. (laughter) It's standing on the corner. It can't speak English...I can't even talk the way these people talk. "Why you ain't where you is go, ra,"... And I blamed the kid until I heard the mother talk. (laughter) Then I heard the father talk. This is all in the house. You used to talk a certain way on the corner and you got into the house and switched to English. Everybody knows it's important to speak English except these knuckleheads. You can't land a plane with "why you ain't..."...

We've got to hit the streets, ladies and gentlemen...look at the Black Muslims. There are Black Muslims standing on the street corners...and we're laughing at them because they have bean pies and all that, but you don't read "Black Muslim gunned down while chastising drug dealer."...Muslims tell you to get out of the neighborhood. When you want to clear your neighborhood out, first thing you do is go get the Black Muslims, bean pies and all. (laughter)...And your neighborhood is then clear.

I'm telling you Christians, what's wrong with you? Why can't you hit the streets? Why can't you clean it out yourselves? It's our time now, ladies and gentlemen. It is our time, (clapping)...It's not about money. It's about you doing something ordinarily that we do get in somebody else's business. It's time for you to not accept the language that these people are speaking, which will take them nowhere. What the hell good is Brown V. Board of Education if nobody wants it?

...this is a sickness ladies and gentlemen and we are not paying attention to these children...They don't know anything...All they know how to do is beg. And you give it to them, trying to win their friendship. And what are they good for? And then they stand there in an orange suit and you drop to your knees, "(crying sound) He didn't do anything, he didn't do anything." Yes, he did do it. And you need to have an orange suit on too. (laughter, clapping)

So, ladies and gentlemen, I want to thank you for the award (big laughter) and giving me an opportunity to speak because, I mean, this is the future, and all of these people who lined up...got to be wondering what the hell happened. Brown V. Board of Education, these people who marched and were hit in the face with rocks and punched in the face to get an education and we got these knuckleheads walking around who don't want to learn English.(clapping) I know that you all know it. I just want to get you as angry as you ought to be...they're dragging me way down because the state, the city and all these people have to pick up the tab on them because they don't want to accept that they have to study to get an education.

We have to begin to build in the neighborhood, have restaurants, have cleaners, have pharmacies, have real estate, have medical buildings instead of trying to rob them all. And so, ladies and gentlemen, please, Dorothy Height, where ever she's sitting, she didn't do all that stuff so that she could hear somebody say "I can't stand algebra, I can't stand...and "what you is." It's horrible.

(Bill Cosby | Pound Cake Speech, 2004)

I am sure you now recall Cosby's *Pound Cake Speech;* or at least read about it. In some ways it speaks to the usual dichotomy within the educated Black person's mental experience. In its most organic form, it is the understanding of Black struggle, but also the frustrations that can arise due to the self deprecating tactics that now seem routine among some Black people. The reality is that Black people in America are forced within the depths of two worlds. One from the East (Africa) and the other is from the West (America). It can be a confusing existence and oftentimes booby trapped in ways where many Blacks are unable to thrive. There was a time when Blacks were forced into unity. That provided more of a communal vision toward progress. As Black elite have ascended into various directions, the larger Black community has lost its way. Some privileged Blacks remain connected to the struggle as an asset, while others rest on their laurels or even develop contempt for Black masses. The latter becomes a disastrous pawn within the established system.

The challenges stemming from the lack of Black unity also affect Black relationships. Instead of having a grip on our history and unique relationship circumstances, news media, scandals, statistics, and social hyperbole pester fragile and already pessimistic expectations. Black women and men are not adequately in touch with each other. There has always been promiscuous, physical, and emotional tomfoolery within some Black relationships. And there will always be relationships with serious challenges. But many Black relationships no longer uphold family traditions of love, respect, and endurance that once sustained us despite the odds.

Many educated Black women have become desensitized to America's systemic daggers that cripple Black love. Not knowing who to blame, many cast the complete onus on Black men. Hurt people hurt people; especially those closest. Advancement requires relationship specific understanding and action as a requirement among educated Black women (and men). Task specific work helps to attract and empower Black relationship longevity. To view the situation from a victim standpoint sustains a victim mentality. That is no good. Not that the majority of educated Black women necessarily do that. But, I am sure you know a few who may. Once again unfair or grievous circumstances are thrust upon educated Black women. God never promised that academic or career excellence would flow ubiquitously upon a love life. Again, it takes task specific work, development, understanding, action, and faith. The reality is that Blacks together, and individually, face circumstantial and gender specific challenges both new and unfinished. Uniting to find solutions will equip Black communities and relationships to stand strong. Divided, the Black community and Black relationships will continue to fall.

Cosby was at times insensitive in his *Pound Cake Speech*, especially when considering his own personal and educational challenges as written in Michael Dyson's *Is Bill Cosby Right? Or Has the Black Middle Class Lost Its Mind?* But many themes of his chastisement were not without some painful realities. Those realities came across in his substance and the recklessness in which he arrived at some of his points. Cosby and all Black Americans, regardless of their economic status, today possess *The Audacity of Hope* because of social and political struggles of our ancestors. Therefore there is a duty to be sensitive to the overall push toward Black progress and make a contribution to it. To ignore this responsibility and operate ignorantly or selfishly is what now happens too often. The results are not good.

School Daze

Formal education is a natural prerequisite for the workforce. Possessing formal education however, is not enough to adequately contribute to Black mass concerns. Do not get me wrong. If you do not have formal education, you need to push toward completing a college degree. A college degree is becoming necessary to get basic employment. If you cannot help yourself it is hard to help the community. But in this section, I am specifically focused on how an understanding beyond formal education can provide a greater contribution to Black progress. A comprehensive understanding of laws and politics that fuel our contemporary environment is essential; and most importantly a desire to seek equality for all people.

Individual achievement is necessary to further the team. But to individually be as bad (good) as Mike (Jordan or Jackson) in 1987, if the team in your corner loses, appears selfish and lacks the political punch felt from *The Greatest: Muhammad Ali*. Individually Mike proved to be invincible and known throughout the world for his swagger and power when on center stage. But he had to do more than jam to arouse this global appeal. Although he had been balling with teams of five since childhood, it was around 1995-1996 that he made history. Why? Mike had matured and learned to merge his personal ambition with a larger and more comprehensive mission. He had learned from the ridicule and taken the fall despite having personally demoralizing his critics winning every individual accolade imaginable. Finally, he thought about the man in the mirror and realized he must strengthen the *Band of Brothers*. And in the ceremonial final analysis fans echoed his contribution as having risen to being the most valuable player ever. Of course the team lives as maybe the greatest dynasty ever and Mike forever immortalized as king.

Highly ranked colleges are marketed to provide an egalitarian situation for anyone able to gain entry. Relevant to Blacks is the fact that most have traditionally forbade proportionate numbers of Black scholars and students entry due to color politics. Even many colleges that historically allowed some integration usually negated the disadvantages that Black inner city and rural school students faced. The Black students chosen to attend were usually middle class.

These Black students were often not only properly trained to assimilate within White society, but possessed less desire to challenge the illegitimate system. This fact has greatly compromised the potential of a truly elite or relevant education for Black concerns. Instead, many institutions served as a forum which legitimized narrow-minded perspectives and inclusion. There are some exceptions and today bits of evolution. However, Blacks must always keep this fact in mind as they encourage matriculation to and from these institutions. My point is that these educational institutions cannot provide the complete knowledge and perspective
needed for Black people to be their best selves.

Education must go beyond Black thought to adequately navigate American landscapes; but it should not be done without considering the Black experience. Yes, each individual should cease what they believe to be the best opportunities presented for growth; opportunities can be multifaceted in their interpretation. The point is that many Black kids receiving education in predominately White environments are beginning to largely grow up without Black neighborhoods, organizations, schools, and sometimes even churches as their foundation. This can result in little meaningful connection, respect, or obligation to understand or contribute to Black uplift beyond themselves. Saving themselves is worth something, but it also has potential to come with a negative residual effect depending on how it is done (Many of these kids can grow up with serious identity problems). The fact that highly ranked institutions now split the community from many of the brightest Black students that once would have attended institutions like *Howard, Tuskegee, FAMU, A&M, Tennessee State, Morehouse,* and *Bennett College* is worth close examination. Because no matter the area code of your Black experience, old White men that dominate as faculty members around the country are fundamentally incapable of training Black students' minds for what they will encounter. Black people must always keep this in perspective as we formulate our value on matriculation to and from the various institutions now available. Not necessarily because we should not leave to attend, but because we should never forget our way back.

Bill Cosby has always done a remarkable job at exemplifying his support for Black colleges by financial contributions and wearing their t-shirts at every turn. Unfortunately Black colleges are not gaining adequate support. Learning institutions like *Fisk, Knoxville College, Charles Drew Medical School,* and others many times struggle like public housing, schools, and streets named after Black civic leaders to serve as institutions synonymous with excellence. Without distinguished communal opportunities for our own Black scholars, they are at the mercy of White publishers and institutions that often dictate their voices and contributions to Black people. Instead of a strengthened educational agenda we are continually subjected to culturally biased entrance exams, education, and legacies. We obviously need stronger preparation so that formal credentials coupled with a cultural knowledge base thrusts Black students into the global, educational, political, and social marketplaces. This way it will be done in a manner where they will always praise *The Souls of Black Folks.*

Imagine the impact on our communities if we all gave a little something to Historically Black Colleges and Universities whether we attended one or not (money, expertise, consulting, time, resources). These institutions need us more than ever, and with over one hundred still in existence, can provide a tremendous service to our future. We have got to begin understanding that the value of investing in ourselves is priceless.

Monster In-Law
Relationship with In-Laws

It is likely that you will feel as if your in-laws, or potential in-laws, are crazy. Not necessarily clinically diagnosed crazy, but crazy just the same. This is mainly for the reasons that irritate you about your man. The only difference is that his dose you have learned to manage in a variety of ways. You have also had ample time to calculate the upside of your relationship with your man. Those in-laws though –goodness! They can weigh on you like Star Jones before the surgery, and do things to cut you to the white meat! Their shortcomings will feel like your man's to the hundredth power. Do not initially expect him to overly sympathize with your feelings about his family. Not only because he is one of them, but because it is hard for anyone to accept an outsider critiquing their family. Yep, for a good long while you will be the outsider. The fact is that his family has been present for him his entire life. They have made him who he is. You have been there a fraction of that time with hopes of reaping the good which they have sewn within him. You must be careful. Too much nagging or mishandling of this situation will have you back on blackpeoplemeet.com with the quickness.

Do not be surprised if his family is judgmental of you. Especially if you are not from their neck of the woods, do not look like them, or are from a different socio-economic background. Most specifically this judgment will be felt from his mother. Possibly from his sister too since you are a bit unlucky. It may be blatant if they are the crunk type; or it could simply trickle to you in glances, phrases, and other idiosyncrasies. They may never feel your truth which is that you are the best thing that ever happened to their son. Despite the fact that you were chosen by him to be a part of the family, mother bear is suspicious of the various agendas women have in courtship and marriage. And maybe that is fair. Tread lightly. She will set the tone for his family's perception and interactions with you.

It is best to allow all in-law relationships to gradually strengthen over time. Be very nice, obviously courteous, and thoughtful. Do not be desperate for their approval. The standard of treatment at the beginning, like in any relationship, will be a strong predictor of your treatment in the future. Eventually, kids may come into play and make things a bit more amicable, but not always.

Do not make the mistake of being lulled in by the niceties of in-laws to the point of actually thinking they love you as much as their son. This mistake only happens if you are desperate for their approval or you truly believe in miracles. Either way, it will most likely make you moreso easy prey. Most mothers think their son could do better than you. Without careful navigation subtle tensions can quickly become almost unbearable. Be cool, be fun, be open, but do not be stupid. The in-laws are watching your every move. It is best to trust that the mother in-law had her hand on the trigger waiting for any woman your man brought through the door. So challenges with you are not necessarily personal. But it will feel that way. The fact that she recognizes you as too tall, short, dark, light, bourgeois, ghetto, fat, skinny, young, old, plain, hoochie, or with limited abilities compared to Suzy Homemaker is unfortunately how the game goes. How you play it will set the table for your future success.

It is very possible that your mother in-law could be single, and may be jealous of the fact that there is the potential for a new number one woman in her son's life. She could be in your hubby's ear with all types of games and sob stories. Remember, his mother for a while will remain the most important woman in his life. Do not forget that point. Unless there has been something tremendous that exposes his mom as a culprit you do not have a chance at being chosen over her (Even then maybe not). Quoting scriptures that say to leave and cleave will not mean anything. It will take substantial time before you become numero uno over momma. Do not get overly frustrated, possessive, or try to keep him away from his mother. But do not let your mother in-law handle you like a pup either. Here are a few tips:

1) *Friendly* –Act friendly, but do not force a friendship.
2) *Polished* –Stay polished (hair done, nails done, etc.).
3) *Thoughtful* –Remain thoughtful and courteous (bring a dish if invited to a meal).
4) *Calm* –Do not argue with your beau in front of the in-laws period. They molded him, so their thoughts are usually in agreement with his. Plus, they simply do not want to see you handling him.
5) *Confident* –Be confident, not cocky.

You are marrying into a family. So get a grip on if you are comfortable with your babies possibly looking and acting like his uncle Joombug based of genetics. Are you really prepared to spend holidays and special moments in the company of these people? Be real with yourself because it will be a part of the deal. Everybody's family has issues, including your own. Do not get so holy when assessing the fact that his family does too. Always be empathetic to the reality that this is their son, baby, and maybe the pride of the family. They made him into the man that you love. His family releasing him to the next phase of life will be a process to be handled gingerly.

Closing

I appreciate you reading these letters. There is obviously so much more to say on many of these topics. Hopefully my letters will spur on conversations, book clubs, self analysis, and spiritual focus. There are more letters to come, since I am an avid writer of my reflections. I do hope that you will read me again or consult with me on questions specific to your situation. I am sure to continuously gain inspiration and perspective from the feedback of educated Black women and others that further my thoughts, and speak to the forever evolving dynamics of relationships.

The next book, *Dear Mr. Educated Black Man*, will expand on old relationship challenges and be about new stuff. Of course, more of the sections will focus on how Black men can get themselves tight. But, I will examine the growing number of Black women considering a sperm bank to have a child, health & fitness, prenups, domestic abuse, moving-in together, blended families, and why so few Black men are in church. These topics impact Black relationships as a whole. Be sure to look out for the book's release. Until next time, praise God, be nice, stay beautiful, get paid, and move toward living *Your Best Life*.

Read next an excerpt from the book, *Dear Mr. Educated Black Man.*

Pretty Woman
Attracting Worthwhile Relationships

My arms hung low and nonchalantly around her waist. But like a vise-grip, the pressure of my hands squeezed the small of her back evenly and sturdy. It was necessary to be convincing but not overzealous. This flick would be seen by millions. I had not known her before yesterday. But it is called the Method technique to be very present in a scene. Despite not being a seasoned professional–I had learned to pull from life experiences to stimulate natural actions and reactions. Let me backtrack.

She looked like a shoo-in for shutting down the scene, but with no experience with big country boys that smile soft but play hard. Despite her cat eyes, five-foot-nine stature, Dark Chocolate Martini colored skin (shaken, not stirred), and Russian Red MAC lipstick that her succulent lips smeared beyond the framework of mine, the details about this Ms. Apple-bottom runner-up from the mid-west is a blur. I do remember clearly however our spontaneous introduction. And it was a bit judgmental the way her eyes dissected my style, smile, and shoe size. I had not treated her like that. But without obvious qualms in which to contest the casting director's choice of our pairing, she offered an ostentatious jab from thirty feet. The fact that she said it arrogantly in front of the whole crew is what made her comment stank instead of a fresh reminder. "Be sure yo breath don't stink!" Laughs from the crew followed. I get it. It would be a kissing scene on film. But to come at me foul without easing close enough to smell the caramel bliss of the Werther's Original that clanged about my teeth damaged my ego and set a standard. I came to find out that it was not the standard she preferred. Men lose when they start sparring with well kept women in public. I knew that. Plus I could not lose this gig! Because... I was a young buck that needed the doe. I would have to be patient. So I resisted the yearning to suggest the cat walk of Hollywood Boulevard or The Moonlit Bunny Ranch as the most lucrative positioning for her services. The response would have been bold, but the kind of no-nonsense rebuttal that this particular woman would have conformed to. Mos Def's song *Ms. Fat Booty* offered Scene 2, and a similar verse would play out the next day. I will get to that. In the moment I was forced to just inhale her insult that hurried out between the double-mint flavors of her gums smacking. But she had miscalculated her mark. I was not that John. Instead, I would have related more with Don "Magic" Juan. She came to find that out. Instead of wifely type respect, she had provoked my eyes to steady on her with intentions that sheepishly smiled everything off. The reality show of that moment finished without contest, but the story was just beginning. I knew that tomorrow would offer only *Fifty Shades of Grey* in this relationship saga. Since she had worked overtime to upgrade her first contract in this PG-13 film we were featured extras on, I would be dominating the terms of the second one.

It is said that within five seconds of an introduction significant impressions surrounding romantic attractiveness are established between people. Of this young lady, my impression was set. From there, my mind and body would only yield to her in a manner that accommodated the standard she had established. It was not my first rodeo; although reality is that she only inspired this mostly cock and bull story.

Who we are at our core will be showcased by our actions, reactions, and values in daily life. That does not mean that all an individual embodies is always apparent. Or that we are not continually evolving and growing into better people. But, progress takes effort. What I am suggesting is that the level of respect, love, and companionship attracted as an adult is largely determined by our perceptions of self and others; this is ultimately what we take in and put out into the world. It is often difficult to see ourselves clearly. Therefore, many of us do not accurately understand the nuances of what we are projecting into the world. How, where, why, and when we put ourselves out there usually correlates directly to what we are attracting. Life challenges can harden us to the point of having an attitude or disposition out of line with our best selves. It may even be a defense mechanism from being hurt or feeling inadequate. For men, it is usually necessary for them to pipe down their little ego, and gain perspective and Godly values that equip them to be *Men of Honor*. Women must cool down, cheer up, and invest in biblical texts that empower them to shun an *Indecent Proposal* if they are preparing to be *Married with Children*.

Each of us must take responsibility for our own impressions, personality, actions, and spirituality. In doing so, we will be aligning ourselves with God's will for our lives. We all have the capacity to improve and attract someone that is special. It requires using the prep-time before entering a relationship to practice Biblical obedience. Once that obedience is rooted inward, it can be an attribute to a healthy relationship. Your relationship can only be as good as you are, and what you attract. When opportunity is upon you to help create a sustainable relationship, there is little time to then get ready. Trust that as you continually seek God, he will provide you the wherewithal to be god-like, and flush out the impurities that keep you bound. *Trust in the Lord with all your heart and lean not on your own understanding; in all your ways submit to him, and he will make your paths straight.* (Proverbs 3:5-6)

Okay, day 2. "Are we to use our tongue when kissing?" Her question was reasonable, but, with no measure of how to place parameters around our $50 upgraded salaries for the day. Plus this was just a rehearsal. "No, they don't pay me enough for all that," I said, with an indignant smirk to serve machismo with my response. But, what I knew my reaction confirmed in her mind was…